UP YOUR EFFECTIVENESS

Your versatile guide to innovative communication

by
JUDY RIGGENBACH

Final editing by Susan R. Quinn,
S.R.K., Denver, Colorado

Illustrations by Regina Hogan

Communication Dynamics
P.O. Box 1461
Wheat Ridge, Colorado 80034

KENDALL/HUNT PUBLISHING COMPANY
Dubuque, Iowa

Copyright © 1984 Judy A. Riggenbach

Library of Congress Catalog Card Number: 82-073358

ISBN 0-8403-3281-5

All rights reserved. No part of this publication may be reproduced, stored in a retrieval system, or transmitted, in any form or by any means, electronic, mechanical, photocopying, recording, or otherwise, without the prior written permission of the copyright owner.

Printed in the United States of America

B 403281 01

This publication is the result of many years of experience. It is sold with the understanding that the author is not engaged in rendering psychological or medical services. If such expert assistance or counseling is needed, the services of a competent professional should be sought.

Dedication —
 to Si, Ruth, Karen, Bee and Cheryl

IMPRESSIONS, be they first or final, are dependent wholly upon communications, verbal or silent. Our ability to cope with and master the world about us is much dependent on the way we communicate with those around us. This is obvious in the world of sales and business, but it is also true in every other aspect of our lives. No one would argue that communication is not every bit as important in our social aspirations. Effective communications begin at birth and continue to our last breath. It is thus the purpose of this book to help us make the most of our communication facilities and increase our effectiveness.

Judy Riggenbach has been active in teaching communication skills for over a decade. She has been tremendously successful in bringing seminars on the subject to thousands. Her credits are impressive. Now she brings her wealth of information to you in this lively, readable, yet informative book, designed to UP YOUR EFFECTIVENESS in all that you strive to achieve. She has taken the latest in scientific research and presented it in a way that is both easy to understand and practical to your everyday use. Unless you are a hermit, having no confrontation with other people at all, you will benefit from Judy Riggenbach's book, UP YOUR EFFECTIVENESS.

Dr. O.J. Seiden
Contributing Editor

PREFACE

A book on communication can never be complete, because the processes are continually growing.

In reading this book you will find a hodgepodge of information — all relating to how and why we communicate as we do.

Because we are all human and individuals, we respond and react differently in similar situations. Consequently, I have used generalizations to describe particular behavior. NOTHING you will read is carved in stone, placed in cement, or written for posterity. You must sift and sort, and use that information which you feel comfortable applying to your unique situations.

UP YOUR EFFECTIVENESS will help you gain the insight needed to communicate more effectively and assuredly with business associates, friends, and family.

JUDY RIGGENBACH

CONTENTS

one .... **Personality Types** 1
                         Extroverts
                         Introverts
                         Ambiverts

two .... **Food and Personality** 17
                         Carrot Eaters
                         Tea Drinkers
                         Cottage Cheese Lovers
                         Meat Addicts
                         Fish Fans

three .... **Weather and Personalities** 21
                         Mood Changes
                         Stress Agitator
                         Physical Effects
                         Emotional Effects

four .... **Stress** 25
                         Causes
                         Effects
                         Coping Tools
                         Workaholics
                         Anxiety Index
                         Fun Stress
                         Women & Stress
                         Teenage Stress

five .... **Burnout or Burnup?** 57
                         Physical
                         Social
                         Intellectual
                         Emotional
                         Spiritual

six . . . . **Life Destinations** 63
　　　　　　　　　Goal Setting
　　　　　　　　　Career Changes

seven . . . . **Coping vs. Escaping** 71
　　　　　　　　　Overeating
　　　　　　　　　Undereating
　　　　　　　　　Alcoholism

eight . . . . **Non-Verbal Communication** . . 79
　　　　　　　　　Body Language
　　　　　　　　　Touch
　　　　　　　　　The Stalls
　　　　　　　　　Eyes
　　　　　　　　　Power
　　　　　　　　　Listening

nine . . . . **Psychological Effects** 131
　　　　　　　　　of Color
　　　　　　　　　Stress and Color
　　　　　　　　　Animals and Color
　　　　　　　　　Moods and Color
　　　　　　　　　Personalities and Color

ten . . . . **I'd Pick More Daisies** 139

one
PERSONALITY TYPES

Communication with others is difficult at best. It isn't too hard to talk to people, but do they understand what we are trying to tell them? Miscommunication is easy. Getting our ideas across to effectively influence what we want done . . . well, that's another matter.

Before you can deal effectively with others you must come to grips with yourself . . . know yourself . . . understand who and what you are, where you are going, how you are going to get there, why you react and respond the way you do. Let's start by determining who you are, extrovert, introvert, or ambivert. Each personality type responds differently as a situation occurs. The category you fall into has no relevance pertaining to your success, but does have an impact on your longevity, as you will see in later chapters.

As you get to know yourself better, you will be able to understand personality conflicts as well as positive relationships. An immediate clue to your personality is how quickly you complete the following inventory. Extroverts will finish the Inventory rapidly, whereas the introvert will take time with detail.

Directions: If your answer is "yes," encircle "yes"; if "no," encircle "no"; if "sometimes," encircle "S". As you read the questions, don't dwell on your answers; simply circle your immediate response.

Yes S No   1. Would you rather stay home and read a good book than go out with a group of friends?

Yes S No   2. Do you like to do jobs carefully and thoroughly, even when a less perfect job would be all right?

Yes S No   3. When you are going to buy something fairly expensive, do you look around carefully before buying?

Yes S No   4. Do you like to do arithmetic problems?

Yes S No   5. Have you lost out in something you wanted to do by not making up your mind quickly enough?

Yes S No   6. Do your friends think you are particular about details?

Yes S No   7. Would you like to have things more settled and safe in your life — with nothing to worry about as you look ahead?

Yes S No   8. Do you like to make minor repairs or adjustments on autos, appliances, or about the house?

Yes S No   9. Does your mind frequently dwell on things you would like to see, do and have?

Yes S No   10. Are you in the clouds one day while "down in the depths" another day?

Yes S No   11. Do you tend to blush easily?

Yes S No   12. Are you careful not to lend money to acquaintances unless you are sure of their honesty?

Yes S No   13. Do you allow people to crowd ahead of you in line?

Yes S No   14. Have you ever been afraid of losing a job because your work went badly?

Yes S No   15. Does it annoy you to have someone watch you at work?

Yes S No   16. Can you keep on doing tiresome, routine work over a long period of time?

Yes S No   17. Are you inclined to keep quiet when out with people you do not know well?

Yes S No   18. Does it annoy you to have people talk about you?

Yes S No   19. Do you like to read serious books or attend lectures?

Yes S No   20. Do you have strong religious or political convictions?

Yes S No   21. Do you have a strong desire to feel more certain of yourself and to be more self-confident?

Yes S No   22. Do you question the wisdom of your decisions after you have made them?

Yes S No 23. Do you like to take care of the details of your work?

Yes S No 24. Do you come right to the point with what you have to do, regardless of the consequences?

Yes S No 25. Do you find people so opinionated that it is hard to reason with them?

Yes S No 26. Do even the most dramatic of your experiences generally leave your personality much the same?

Yes S No 27. In the organizations to which you belong, are you usually satisfied to be a member rather than one of the leaders?

Yes S No 28. Can you express yourself orally more easily than in writing?

Yes S No 29. Do you remember people well?

Yes S No 30. Are you inclined to exaggerate about your experiences or about what you can do?

Yes S No 31. Are you usually late for an appointment?

Yes S No 32. Is it easy for you to change an opinion or belief?

Yes S No 33. Do you like to be busy with several things at the same time?

Yes S No 34. Do you find it easy to get started with new projects?

Yes S No 35. Are most people willing to co-operate with you and your plans?

Yes S No 36. Do you accept people's mistakes and little annoying actions good-naturedly?

Yes S No 37. When you are out with two or three friends, are you usually the one who decides where to go and what to do?

Yes S No 38. Do you like to have power or influence over people, so you can make them do as you wish?

Yes S No 39. Are you quick to say what you feel like saying, compared to other people?

Yes S No 40. Are you inclined to go ahead and do things without thinking much about the outcome?

Yes S No 41. After you have done the big and difficult parts of a job, do you dislike finishing up the odds and ends?

Yes S No 42. Have other people told you that you are a proud, stuck-up, or egotistical person?

Yes S No 43. Do you laugh readily?

Yes S No 44. Do you care what other people think about you?

Yes S No 45. Do you like to gamble?

Yes S No 46. Do you feel at ease upon entering a room where there are several strange people?

Yes S No 47. Do people say you are a person who will have his own way?

Yes S No 48. Do you prefer jobs where you work with other people?

Yes S No 49. Do you speak to people first on meeting them?

Yes S No 50. Are you answering these questions quickly, without much thought or deliberation?

Scoring:

Count two points for each "yes" answer circled between numbers 1 — 27 ONLY.

Count two points for each "no" answer circled between numbers 28 — 50 ONLY.

Count one point for every "S" answer between 1 — 50.

TOTAL YOUR SCORE _____

Check your score: 0-39 puts you into the extroverted category; a score of 40-59 indicates an ambivert personality. (The closer your score is to 39, the more extroverted characteristics you possess; the closer the score is to 60, the more introverted tendencies you show.) A score of 60 or more puts you in the introverted category.

Oftentimes we are put in categories, and that is exactly what this inventory has done. Before we go any further, we must understand that nothing is "written in stone." There are exceptions to everything. Even though you may fall into the extroverted category or the introverted category, you will find you have characteristics of each. The majority of people taking this test will fall in the ambivert category, because most people are a combination of both introvert and extrovert. It doesn't matter which category you are in. Each category has both positive and negative traits. The purpose of the inventory is to give you insight to the characteristics you possess so you can better use those characteristics in dealing with the people you live and work with. You can better relate to others knowing how you and they react and respond in various situations.

To show you the difference between the two extremes of introvert and extrovert, picture, if you will, a workshop in a garage. On the wall is a peg board. On the peg board is a picture of a hammer and the hammer is in its place, a picture of a saw and the saw is in its place, a picture of a screwdriver and so on . . . Below the peg board is a bench . . . clean with one exception, a small case containing drawers, with each drawer labeled, "nuts," "bolts," "nails," etc. You go to the drawer marked "nails," what do you find? Of course, nails! because this is the workshop of an introvert. Incidentally, there is no sawdust or dirt on the floor. Everything is spotless. Introverts tend to be detailed and precision people.

Now picture, if you will, another workshop . . . that of the extrovert. Yes, there is a peg board on the wall. There are even pictures of tools on the peg board (painted by an introvert, no doubt, as an extrovert wouldn't take the time to detail the pictures). What do you think is in the place of the pictured hammer? right, a screwdriver, or some rope, or nothing! There is a bench below the peg board . . . heaped . . . the small case with drawers sits atop the mess. If you were to go to the drawer marked "bolts," what would you find? Nails? Screws? Anything? Extroverts tend to be less detailed than introverts. Now you have a partial picture of the two extremes.

Often, due to career requirements, an extrovert will become organized and an introvert less organized. As an example, you may find characteristics from other categories that fit you. You may be an extrovert working with computer programming where the need to be organized is imperative; therefore, you have changed and adapted to the organization.

One way to tell a true introvert from a true extrovert is to open the top drawer of a desk. An introvert will have a place for everything: paper clips, rubberbands, erasers, pencils, pens, pads, staples, etc. The extrovert's will look as if he — ("he" in this book refers to people, not a specific sex) — simply tossed in everything imaginable. Another way to differentiate between the two is to look at the top of the desk. What will the top of an introvert's desk look like? A telephone . . . notepad and pen . . . whatever appears will be clean and tidy. An extrovert? Definitely heaped. This is not to say extroverts can't find what they are looking for or that they're unduly disorganized. They normally know where everything is . . . their work areas just look disheveled.

Another visible difference between the personalities is the way people walk. An introvert will take his time in getting where he is going, an extrovert will rush and bounce along. This could be one reason why introverts and extroverts sometimes have difficulty getting along. The extrovert says, "Come on, let's go," the introvert says, "Don't rush. Let's move with caution!"

It is said that the majority of introverts come from rural areas and that the majority of extroverts come from urban areas. Why? Living in the "fast lane" may have something to do with that. As an example, try to get on an elevator in New York City . . . if you were to approach the situation as an introvert, you might never achieve your purpose. However, in approaching the elevator as an extrovert, pushing, shoving and being assertive, the task is somewhat easier. (This is not to say that all extroverts push, shove, etc., or that all extroverts come from urban areas. We are speaking of majorities.) In rural areas people are more accustomed to being alone, working alone, and entertaining themselves, rather than dealing with the masses.

Introverts usually get along best with other introverts, extroverts with other extroverts, and ambiverts with other ambiverts. The old saying that "opposites attract" can be true, but it's not necessarily the most comfortable or logical situation. An introvert in the same household or work situation with an extrovert can be extremely disrupting, and vice versa, as one tends to be logical, and precise, the other emotional and disheveled.

As you can see, subtle differences occur between personalities on varied levels. The more overt characteristics are defined in the following paragraphs.

The behavioral traits discussed in the following paragraphs will help you in determining how to better communicate with others.

The introvert expresses emotions inwardly, is concerned with causes and analyses of action, prefers detailed, painstaking work and does not care to work with others as much as he cares to see the results of his own efforts. Introverts tend toward such professions as scientists, inventors, engineers and accountants.

The extrovert expresses emotions outwardly and is more concerned with action than with causes. The inclination is to put ideas into action without giving much consideration to the possible effects of such action. Extroverts gravitate to professions such as politics, sales, athletics, and acting.

The ambivert is a balance of the two extremes and is usually able to adjust more easily and readily to life's problems than either the introvert or extrovert. Likewise, he is usually more successful in dealing with people. The ambivert manager, wife, father, and boss is easy to get along with and understands both sides of the question. He is more successful in dealing with people.

Now, let's be more specific concerning the differences between personalities of the introverts and extroverts. (Remember, ambiverts, you fall in between.) An introvert will express emotions inwardly, internalizing feelings. The introvert is the one who gets and keeps ulcers. He is a worrier; when an introvert has nothing to do he will worry . . . "What should I do today? I think I'll worry." The other extreme, the extrovert, doesn't worry enough. Actually, one of the few times he worries is when he feels guilty about not worrying!

Introverts are concerned with causes and analysis of actions. This is where the detail and patience comes in. In a sales situation, the introvert is interested in detail, facts and benefits. As a manager, his interests are in detail, clean desks, and perfection. An introvert will respond to the written word better, in that he can see and analyze information. The extrovert in the same situation will react emotionally. He will make an instantaneous decision and think about it later, and perhaps change his mind at that time. Usually when an introvert makes a decision, he will stick by it.

The introvert does not like to lend money or possessions. If you borrow a book from an introvert, on the front cover will be: name, street address, zip code, county, state, phone number and directions on how to get the book back to him. The extrovert, on the other hand, loves to loan things out, but never seems to remember where they are.

Extroverts get frustrated with this trait and often promise themselves that they will make note of whom they loan to . . . but being extroverts they never seem to do this. There are probably several extroverts reading this book now who will loan it out before finishing it and then will wonder where it could be.

Introverts prefer to prepare a report in writing rather than verbalize. They tend to be more bashful in front of a crowd than extroverts. In fact, introverts, before giving an oral report or speech will either hyperventilate, throw up, or get diarrhea, while the extroverts enjoy getting up before groups . . . love the applause and attention. Some extroverts do experience nervousness; they just don't mind it as much.

An introvert is usually outspoken in his views and opinions, especially concerning religion, money, and politics. It is very difficult to win an argument with an introvert. He argues just to argue. An extrovert feels others have a right to their opinions, and will let it go at that. The introvert will spend much time trying to prove his is the only way . . . trying to change your mind. In fact, it has been said that an introvert uses argument as an intellectual exercise. The extrovert does not want to take the time to argue.

The extrovert normally seems rushed. He will set his watch ahead ten minutes, so he can be on time, but very rarely makes the deadline. An introvert will be early, or on time, and very aware of deadlines.

An introvert does not easily laugh. Once again he internalizes emotions, lets them build up and finally explodes. The extrovert is the one heartily laughing, kicking tires and pounding desks . . . releasing emotion everywhere and releasing stress, a major cause of the introvert's ulcers, headaches, backaches, etc. The extrovert is not easily embarrassed, whereas the introvert blushes readily.

The introvert will take particular care of personal property. Like the desk drawer with everything in place, the introvert wants everything just so, from home to office, to car, to family. An introvert likes to tinker, polish, and adjust his personal property, whereas an extrovert appreciates having it done for him.

The introverts are generally bashful with the opposite sex and prefer to keep their own counsel, hence the internalizing of emotions. The extroverts are gregarious, not bashful, and love to talk. Extroverts will talk your ear off and be overtly enthusiastic, making it difficult for you to get a word in.

Introverts do not move quickly in the routine actions of the day, such as talking, dressing, walking, etc. This is one area where introverts and extroverts drive one another crazy. The extrovert is anxious to get on with action and the introvert is satisfied taking time, caution, double checking.

Concerning perfection, when you receive a letter from an introvert it will probably have been rewritten at least three times. Perfection is a key to the introvert's personality, not only in letter writing, but in all aspects. The extrovert, on the other hand, in writing a letter, will cross words out, write in the margins, and always will have that afterthought — a "p.s.," if not on the letter, on the sealed envelope!

The introvert is extremely sensitive to criticism. If you tell one you don't like his tie or her dress, you may never see the garment again. Tell that to an extrovert and he or she will say, "Hey, if you don't like it, don't look at it. That's your problem, not mine!" It is difficult to hurt the feelings of the extrovert. That is not to say he is insensitive, but he will handle criticism better than the very sensitive introvert.

The introvert dislikes being ordered to do things, whereas the extrovert has to be reminded. An introvert knows he can get it done, doesn't need to be told, in fact resents being told.

The introvert will struggle along with a problem, rather than ask for help. Let's say you're going to a new restaurant for dinner and the introvert is driving. Your reservations are for 8:00. It is now 7:45 and the driver (introvert) is still trying to find the street. He'll drive until 9:00 trying to find it. He will not ask for help! If the driver were an extrovert, he would have stopped at the first gas station and asked directions. Be aware of the introvert in your home or business who may be *struggling* with an *unnecessary* problem.

Introverts are moved to best efforts by praise, compliments and stroking. Extroverts, too, respond to praise, but not as much as introverts.

You may find the introvert very suspicious of the motives of others. One must prove himself to the introvert before trust is accepted. An extrovert will trust nearly everyone.

An introvert is an unlikely gambler, with money or ideas. He must know and understand all the facts, then proceed. If an introvert were to go to Las Vegas with $50, he'd probably return with $49. The extrovert with $50 would either have to borrow money to get home or come home with thousands. The extrovert takes chances and risks. The introvert learns to live with moodiness . . . the roller coaster ride of emotions . . . he is frequently up and down. The exterior will be up most of the time; however, about twice a year the extrovert will fall into the depths of depression. There is nothing worse than an extrovert in the pits . . . he just doesn't know how to handle himself. It is his inclination to bring everyone down with him. My suggestion for an extrovert in the pits is to lock himself in a closet for about three days and wallow in self pity. He shouldn't bring everyone down with him! Introverts . . . just ignore that extrovert who appears somewhat moody . . . he will soon get over it!

Keep in mind that it doesn't matter which category you fall into, but that you need to be aware of how different personalities will react to you and to your personality.

And remember, the ambivert will have dual characteristics, but not as pronounced as the extrovert or introvert. Know yourself. Know under what conditions you function best. Plan your strategy so that you use the characteristics of others in your own favor.

Think about situations you've been in . . . the personalities of the people in those situations. How might you have handled the situation differently knowing about personality differences?

two
**FOOD
AND
PERSONALITY**

Studies at the Tokyo Food Research Institute, Columbia University, University of London, and U.S. Department of Defense, have revealed a correlation between a person's food preferences and mental abilities and personality traits. When we eat, we communicate. The way in which we ingest food, gobble, slurp, inhale, crunch, pig out, savor, devour, nibble, relish, indicates attitudes and personalities. A person's disposition, as well as his/her earning power may well be the result of what is eaten. The key is to determine the food you will select *when given a choice*. If you are dieting and must eat a certain diet, chances are the correlating personality traits will not be accurate.

It has been found that:

- Carrot eaters are generally more sociable.

- Spinach eaters are easy to get along with.

- Cottage cheese lovers are subject to mood changes.

- Tea drinkers live longer and are generally more refined than non-tea drinkers.

- Rutabaga eaters are more conservative.

Concerning personality traits, it has been found that those who prefer fish, fruits, and vegetables tend to be more reserved, quiet in temperament, prefer to work alone, perform well on assignments requiring attention to detail, prefer art, books, music, and are not as competitive as meat eaters. Recognize the introvert?

Big meat eaters, especially those with a strong preference for steak, usually like direct action, exhibit initiative, possess enthusiasm, have a zest for action, are sociable, make good leaders, salespeople, corporation officers, and politicians. Any correlations between this and the extrovert?

Those who are fond of bread, potatoes, pasta, in fact any starchy foods, may be adverse to solving problems.

People who tend to work at a brisk pace, speak fast, write short letters, are sympathetic and willing to listen to other's problems, are the salad lovers.

Dessert lovers tend to be impulsive, with strong commanding personalities, even more so than the meat eaters, and have a lively sense of humor.

Anyone feeling a need to have milk and/or ice cream with meals may suffer from feelings of insecurity and subconsciously want to retreat to childhood.

Those who like most foods will be energetic, assertive, affectionate, sociable, have a love of comfort and relaxation, have dominant personalities, and will be able to communicate their feelings freely.

It has also been found that people project many of their basic problems and anxieties, such as phobias, obsessions, complexes and defenses, into their eating habits.

You are what you eat!

three
WEATHER AND PERSONALITIES

You will find that the weather has an effect on behavioral patterns, attitudes and moods. Tomorrow's forecast can predict how your energy, health and job performance will be affected. The effect that weather has will increase if you are not used to the particular pattern of the area you are now living in. For example, if you live in a humid climate, then the hot, humid conditions will have less effect on you than if you lived in a dry area and newly experienced the humidity.

Our moods are often determined by the weather conditions of the past couple of days. There are several signals of sensitivity to weather: bad moods, tiredness, unwillingness to work, head pressure, restless or disturbed sleep, headaches, forgetfulness, listlessness.

Weather creates stress, and changes in the weather can affect your stress levels. Drastic changes in the weather affects the body chemistry and oxygen supply to the brain, which in turn can alter moods and behavior. During storms and just before, our behavior changes more than any other time. Before a storm children tend to become unruly, adults edgy and more accidents will occur. People will be more forgetful, unbalanced, and become more violent. Suicides increase right before a storm, as do fainting spells, drunkenness, and insomnia.

During a storm, buyers are more receptive, especially at the point when the barometer begins to rise. Alcohol and drugs are more potent and have a stronger effect during a storm.

After a storm is the time to patch up those quarrels, since people seem to be more receptive, look and feel better.

During warm and humid weather traffic accidents increase, as do family quarrels. This time is not good for mental alertness. Tempers get out of hand, people are irritable, lack concern and don't have a good sense of humor.

If the weather is too hot, people don't think clearly. The months of July and August are peak times for family quarrels, riots, and crimes of violence. Because of the hot temperature during August it is the worst month for testing. People have to be patient with others and control tempers during hot weather.

Moderate cold is mentally stimulating. The months of April and November are great for test-taking.

Rain promotes good physical health (moderate rain), as it takes less effort to do something during rain. There also seems to be increased intelligence and more efficiency during this time.

But remember, in forecasting your moods, it is never just cold, dry, hot, wet or windy alone . . . there are always combinations. Weather influences you with numerous effects, modified by the climate to which you may be accustomed.

Be aware that physical effects are strongest from changes in atmospheric pressure, humidity and the seasons. Mental influence is strongest from heat, cold and wind changes.

Air conditioning has changed the body's tolerance for changing weather conditions. It has been found that people working in air conditioned buildings have more ailments, feel more uncomfortable and have more headaches than those who work in non-air conditioned buildings.

The weather has a definite effect on the communication process through its impact on your attitude and mood.

four
STRESS

As you get to know yourself better, you'll come to understand how the stress in your life affects your communication process with others. You may be experiencing stress symptoms now that you aren't even aware of . . . a nagging backache, that little catch in your neck, fatigue, sore throat, pain in the leg, pain in the knee, pain in the neck. Medical research tells us that over 80% of illness is stress related.

Stress isn't all bad. Without stress, life would become boring. Stress is necessary for motivation. Some people can deal with more stress than others. Some work very effectively under stress and pressure, more so than without it. *IT ISN'T HOW MUCH STRESS YOU ARE UNDER, BUT HOW YOU HANDLE IT THAT COUNTS.*

In this chapter we will analyze how much stress you are experiencing and show effective ways to handle and reduce the stressors in our life.

I hope that after you read this you'll be concerned and moved to lessen the elements that cause you stress and distress. Again . . . *ALL STRESS IS NOT BAD. It is how you cope with it that's important.*

Stress can affect people in many ways: the temperature of your body reduces, due to constriction of the capillaries. Increased capillary fragility causes you to bruise easier. Stress tends to throw off the entire game plan of the body. Emotions, intellectual processes, and social functions are inhibited. I am not referring to the simple stresses we feel and experience every day, but to the long term effects, the stress that logs in our bodies and builds up over a number of years.

Keep in mind that there is both positive and negative stress. We generally think of stress in terms of the negative. We shouldn't. Receiving an award causes positive stress. Happy occasions such as weddings, anniversaries, and birthdays, especially the 30th, 40th and 50th can cause a great deal of stress, even though we think of those occasions as happy events.

Effects of Stress

Even though you do not feel the immediate effects of stress, you will eventually, since it tends to build up in the body. You may think you are handling a situation beautifully, ignoring the anxiety, frustration, anger, but the stress of that moment will log somewhere in your body . . . your lower back . . . neck . . . shoulders . . . head . . . temples . . . eyes . . . Ring a bell? Those stresses will surface in due time in the form of aches and pains, or worse.

Oftentimes when your body is reaching high stress levels it will somehow tell you, i.e., insomnia, irritability, absenteeism, change in appetite, apathy, poor judgment, diminished memory, strained relationships, increased errors, indecisiveness, withdrawal, boredom, decrease in motivation, negativity, dullness, and so forth.

More advanced signs of stress are: excessive daydreaming about doing something different, difficulty in making decisions, increased use of cigarettes and alcohol, sudden outbursts of temper, reversals in usual behavior, excessive worry about unimportant things, forgetfulness, beginning to mistrust friends and family.

Physical signs of stress are evident in the body, i.e., chest pain . . . there is a direct correlation between stress and heart attacks. According to statistics there are more than 4,000 heart attacks per day between the ages of 35 and 40 that are stress-related. Stress also causes hypertension; over 60 million persons in the United States have high blood pressure. Stress has also been known to cause arthritis, rheumatism, colitis, constipation, diarrhea, chronic headache, ulcers, skin rashes, hair loss, vertigo, and of course, nervous breakdown.

The mental effects of stress are shown by depression, fatigue, suicide, alcoholism, drug abuse, physical abuse (child, wife and husband beating). Low productivity is another mental effect of stress, along with absenteeism, accidents, work ineffectiveness, tardiness. People, under a great deal of stress, just don't care. They become non-functional.

Causes of Stress

What causes stress? What causes stress in your life? The causes are different for everyone.

We tend to put ourselves in "boxes" that cause us stress . . . those self-imposed obligations, the desire to "live up to" certain expectations.

The number one "box" or stressor across the U.S. is money. Money, either too much or not enough, causes people more stress than anything else. Money does not buy everything that makes us happy, nor does the lack of it please.

The number two stressor is spouses. Third is kids.

Fourth is job. (Please note the word "career" is not used.) A job causes stress. What's the difference between "job" and "career"? Perhaps a "job" is simply an interim activity, not challenging you or providing you with the happiness, security and creativity, a "career" would. If you are happy in your career, you do not have nearly the stress that a person who is holding a "job" has. A job can be boring, and boredom ranks high among stressors.

Time, too much or too little, is the number five stressor. Have you ever experienced too much time on your hands? What happens to people with too much time? Boredom? Mental stagnation? Unrest? When you're used to a tough schedule, regimented living, then time on your hands can destroy you, as during a vacation. Perhaps this happens more during the retirement years than any other time, when goals have been achieved and not reset.

Stagnation causes feelings of worthlessness and causes stress. Not enough time causes us to push ourselves, become uneasy, and pressure others.

Planning your time can reduce stress. Set a goal. We tend to spend more time planning a three day weekend than we do our lives. A goal will help you relieve stress, now and in later years, in that you'll know where you're going, how you're getting there, and who'll be helping you. (See chapter for life planning ideas.)

Workaholics

The following questionnaire will help you determine how much stress you put on yourself, by indicating whether you are a Type A, workaholic, or Type B person. The Type A's will cause a great deal of stress by putting undue pressure on themselves, by not delegating, doing too many diversified activities, working long hours, drinking gallons of coffee, oftentimes smoking several packs of cigarettes a day, expecting near perfection from others, and expecting as much energy from others as they have themselves.

Type A's seem to have a short fuse which relates closely to heart attack risk. Because Type A wants perfection, he will waste time on trivia and focus on how many people fall short of his perfectionist attitude. This tends to foster hostility and stress. The Type A, being competitive and ambitious, generates negative stress through the continual flow of great amounts of adrenalin in the nervous system, increased by generally poor eating habits. The flow of adrenalin causes a decrease in white cell production, which in turn reduces the body's immune process. This imbalance over a period of time causes deterioration in health, resulting in headaches, colds, back pains, muscle tension, ulcers, infections, and poor healing.

The Type B personality handles life with less anxiety and competitiveness. This person can leave work in the office, relax, take time off, concentrate on one activity at a time, complete activities and generally live a less complicated and longer life.

INSTRUCTIONS: Read each item and make a check next to statements describing habits that are characteristic of you. If the description fits you in general, although not entirely, check the item.

1. I generally move and walk rapidly.

2. I tend to accent key words when I am talking.

3. I eat quickly.

4. I never feel particularly impatient.

5. Sometimes people misunderstand what I say because I speed up my speech at the end of a sentence.

6. If a new gadget comes out or if I see a beautiful piece of bric-a-brac, I like to buy it.

7. I prefer football to baseball because the game moves faster.

8. I schedule my life so that I am hardly ever rushed.

9. A slow driver ahead of me really irritates me.

10. I prefer reading condensations to wading through a whole book.

11. Small talk bores me; I like to talk about things that are important to me.

12. I have equipment in my car for dictating letters and ideas while I drive (or if I do not, I wish I did).

13. I have to read the paper or watch the news while eating a meal.

14. I have a couple of nervous gestures or tics, but they do not bother me much.

15. When I really want to make a point, I am apt to pound on the table.

16. It is hard for me to relax and do nothing. I usually feel guilty if I do not make use of my time.

17. I am never aware of feeling hostile or just plain angry with the world.

18. The prospect of compettion makes me raring to go in there and win.

19. Some of the best solutions to problems at work come to me when I am doing something else, such as playing golf or bridge.

20. I work at a steady pace without making any fuss about it.

21. People often point out things around me that I have not noticed, such as a bird, a flower, or a sunset.

22. It does not bother me a bit when I lose in a game, even if I am pretty good at it.

23. Things often break around me, such as shoe laces, pencil points, and buttons off my clothing, or I grind my teeth.

24. I love to take a vacation and just do nothing.

25. My reports are always in on time or even before they are due; I am efficient in this respect.

26. I enjoy being "one up" on others, especially the people who are trying so hard to get ahead.

27. I get a lot of relaxation from sports, such as a game of tennis, handball, or swimming.

28. I can truly say that it does not bother me to be late to a meeting.

29. My philosophy is: "If you miss the plane, there'll be another one soon — no need to sweat about it."

Give yourself one point for each of the following numbers you checked: 4, 8, 17, 20, 22, 24, 27, 28, 29

A score of 0-4 indicates Type A behavior; a score of 5 and above indicates Type B behavior.

Anxiety Index

There are stress factors not appearing on the above test. Keep in mind that there are many other internal stresses that can add significantly to your stress levels: the weather (hot, humid, windy), diet (excess sugar, cholesterol, fats, caffeine), jealousy, envy, getting even, anger, resentment, fear, loneliness, decision-making or lack of it, being the first born child of a family, no goals, boredom on the job, and all those self-imposed obligations such as having to cook, clean, make a good living, and feeling guilty about taking some time for ourselves.

Often we cannot change the external factors, but most important is the fact that *we can change our reaction* to stressful situations. But first we must recognize those situations which cause us stress, anxiety and distress. As individuals we react differently to like situations.

The following inventories are designed to tell you just how much stress you are now experiencing, and how well you cope with that stress. They will warn you if you do not handle your stress in an effective manner so that instead, you can make your stress work *for* you rather than be counterproductive.

The following categories are rated from mild anxiety-producing conditions to acute stress, if the conditions are not recognized and handled as stress inducors. Check those situations that have occured in your life the past year. Analyze the impact they have had on your emotional and physical stability.

THE ANXIETY INDEX

*by Judy Riggenbach
and
Dr. Othniel J. Seiden*

If the item listed is not a factor in your life, past, present or future, give it a score of 0. If it is relevant to you today, give it a score of 1-5, as you would judge its stressing effect on you PRESENTLY.

1 = mild feeling of irritation
2 = somewhat worrisome, frequent sighing
3 = fairly constant source of worry and aggravation
4 = very irritable, feeling aches and pains, sleep changes, depression and anxiety, habit changes with eating, drinking, smoking and sleeping.
5 = prevents my functioning, unable to cope, notice changes in my personality and body functions

Financial

    a. concern over bankruptcy, past or future
    b. indebtedness
    c. foreclosure
    d. harassment by creditors
    e. family spending irresponsibility
    f. other

Total _____

Occupation

    a. change in job responsibilites
    b. job loss
    c. relationship with fellow workers
    d. promotion
    e. salary reduciton

   f. salary increase
   g. relationship with superiors
   h. job location
   i. distance traveled
   j. job status
   k. insecurity
   l. office politics
  m. job apathy
   n. insecurity about company future
   o. environment
   p. schedule changes
   q. ethics and morals
   r. unreasonable hours
   s. deadlines
   t. job satisfaction
   u. job challenge
   v. other

Total _____

Family Events

   a. change in structure (impending birth, kids moving away, inlaws moving in)
   b. wedding
   c. divorce
   d. separation
   e. death
   f. pets
   g. appearance of spouse/family members
   h. Other

Total _____

Life Style Changes

    a. vacation
    b. holidays
    c. moving
    d. retirement
    e. affair
    f. middle age adjustment
    g. nursing home, self/family member
    h. ethical conflicts
    i. moral conflicts
    j. return to school
    k. religious attitude changes
    l. basic value changes
   m. illness
    n. accidents
    o. other

              Total _____

Responsibilities

    a. decision-making
    b. self-imposed obligations
    c. burdened with responsibilities of others
    d. sole family supporter
    e. too much work, too little time
    f. other

              Total _____

Sex

    a. quantity
    b. quality
    c. variety
    d. too rigid

e. communications
　　f. inhibited
　　g. open-minded
　　h. flexible
　　i. fear
　　j. change in partner
　　k. guilt/morality, religious beliefs
　　l. frustration
　m. self-image
　　n. emotion
　　o. other

Total _____

Legal

　　a. lawsuit
　　b. injustice
　　c. arrest
　　d. litigation
　　e. fine
　　f. jail sentence
　　g. ticket
　　h. IRS
　　i. eviciton
　　j. other

Total _____

Environment

　　a. world events
　　b. economy
　　c. ecology
　　d. home
　　e. politics

    f. moral/ethical/social deterioration
    g. other

                Total _____

Self Concept

    a. physical attributes
    b. attitude toward perfection
    c. dress and grooming
    d. accomplishments
    e. personality
    f. boredom
    g. goal-setting
    h. other

                Total _____

Relationships with

    a. family
    b. parents
    c. kids
    d. spouse
    e. friends
    f. work associates
    g. social groups
    h. affair

                Total _____

Communications

I'm frequently misunderstood by:
    a. parents
    b. spouse
    c. kids

d. friends
e. subordinates
f. superiors
g. other

Total _____

Add up the total points and place score in Box A. ☐ A

Now take the following test and place score in Box B. ☐ B

How Do You Cope?

1. Do you work at a hectic pace that is mostly self-imposed, find you feel guilty when you're not producing and get aggravated when people or things stand in your way from getting more done?

ALWAYS = 3   SOMETIMES = 2   RARELY = 1

2. Do you love your work, truly consider it an adventure rather than a drudgery, a job rather than just a means to make a living?

ALWAYS = 3   SOMETIMES = 2   RARELY = 1

3. Are you able to leave your work at the office and relax with hobbies, sports, friends and family without the worries and aggravations of the job sneaking up on you?

ALWAYS = 1   SOMETIMES = 2   SELDOM = 3

4. I can escape my stress by having a few cocktails, tranquilizers, marijuana, cocaine, or other drugs.

ALWAYS = 1   SOMETIMES = 2   SELDOM = 3

5. I am in total control of my emotions, keeping in my feelings, never yelling or letting off steam, crying or getting outwardly angry.

ALWAYS = 1   SOMETIMES = 2   SELDOM = 3

6. I am constantly disappointed and aggravated by others who never live up to my expectations of them.

ALWAYS = 1   SOMETIMES = 2   SELDOM = 3

7. Do you have specific obtainable goals aimed to satisfy career, life, family, spiritual, community and personal needs?

YES = 3   PARTLY = 2   NO = 1

Now add up the points you've circled above. Place that in Box B.

Box B ☐

Divide that total into the total score of test A. "A" divided by "B" = your index score.

Scoring:

20+ — HIGH STRESS LEVEL   You need to identify your stress generators and find more effective ways to cope with stress.

10 to 19 — HIGH AVERAGE   You are dealing with some aspects of your stress well, but need to continue looking for what generates stress for you and ways to cope more effectively.

5 to 9 — LOW AVERAGE you have probably identified most generators and are coping rather effectively.

1 or less to 4 — LOW You may be very self-assured and comfortable with yourself and your life. However, you may be in the class of people who are unaware of their stress. Remember, the first step in stress management is awareness and realistic acceptance.

Keep in mind that this is only an estimate of your stress levels. Your awareness of anxiety-producing conditions is the key to reducing your stress.

Fun Stress

Oftentimes people question why "Christmas and vacations" is on the stress test. Even though they come and go, these events cause stress which lingers in your body. It is a well-known fact that due to change in climate, eating and sleeping habits, and general routine, a vacation is extremely stressful. People who are accustomed to activity find themselves trying to fill the time. The money spent on vacations is a stressor, even though you might be enjoying it.

Christmas is very depressing and agonizing for some, as suicide statistics show. Self-imposed obligations cause the most stress during the holidays . . . money being spent for gifts, entertaining, unfulfilled expectations, and pretending to be joyful and happy. It has been found that even though you receive the gift you have requested, you won't be totally satisfied, in that the color, size or style won't be quite right. Holidays, joyous as they are, cause anxiety.

One would not want to totally eliminate all stress from life. It is stress that motivates us and keeps life interesting.

In order to reduce stress you must first realize what is causing your stress. Then you must begin to address it somehow. One can't wave a magic wand and eliminate it, but reducing stress will lengthen your life!

Stress-Prone?

To tell if you are a stress-prone personality, rate yourself as to how you typically react in each of the situations listed below. There are no right or wrong answers.

4 - Always
3 - Frequently
2 - Sometimes
1 - Never

1. I try to do as much as possible in the least amount of time.

2. I become impatient with delays or interruptions.

3. I have to win at games to enjoy myself.

4. I find myself speeding up the car to get through amber lights.

5. I hesitate to ask for, or indicate I need help with a problem.

6. I seek the respect and admiration of others.

7. I am critical of the way others do their work.

8. I have the habit of looking at my watch or clock often.

9. I strive to better my position and achievements.

10. I spread myself "too-thin" in terms of time.

11. I have the habit of doing more than one thing at a time.

12. I get angry or irritable.

13. I have time for hobbies or time by myself.

14. I have a tendency to talk quickly or hasten conversations.

15. I consider myself hard-driving.

16. My friends and relatives consider me to be hard-driving.

17. I have a tendency to get involved in multiple projects.

18. I have a lot of deadlines in my work.

19. I feel guilty when I relax and do nothing during leisure time.

20. I take on too many responsibilities.

Total Your Score _____

SCORE: 20-30 Non-productive
30-50 Good balance

Too tense
SCORE: 50-60 Too tense
60 + Good candidate for heart disease

Reducing Stress

There are various coping tools everyone can implement to reduce individual stress levels. It's important to reduce your anxieties, rather than escape from them. Take decisive steps to make positive changes.

1. Learn to plan by setting goals (See Life Destinations Chapter);

2. Exercise, even a little. It can reduce the level of anxiety and provides a socially acceptable form of letting off steam. It builds stamina and reduces the risk of illness.

3. Learn to say "no." The "yes" people have a high correlation to heart attacks.

4. Have a hobby and channel your energies in a relaxing and challenging way. Do something, other than work, that takes your total concentration. A "workaholic" will tell you that work is a hobby. Not so. One must take a break now and then. Incidentally, the workaholic is a happy person; the people around him/her are unhappy, unable to handle the work hours and lack of social contact.

5. Have a positive attitude and count your blessings now and then. It takes more energy to frown than to smile. Negativism causes stress.

6. Learn to relax through meditation or daydreaming. Let your mind wander.

7. Some people drink to reduce stress. This must be considered with caution. (see Chapter Seven).

8. Delegate responsibilities. You don't have to do everything yourself, in your home or in your office.

9. Organization can help reduce stress, through both planning and putting things in perspective. Extroverts are great with this. They will walk into the house one day and clean and clean, and get rid of all those heaps they collect!! Cleaning can be great for the soul.

10. Sex can reduce stress levels in most cases; however in some situations it can cause more stress.

11. Rank your priorities and use the necessary amount of energy for the most important things first.

12. Recognize and accept your limits. Don't try to outdo others.

13. Slow your pace of life. Try not to do so much. Refuse to be obsessed with time, and work at your own pace. Keep your schedule flexible and provide breathing space during the day. Live a day at a time.

14. Recognize that it's normal to make mistakes. Realize that you may learn from mistakes.

15. Learn to have fun. Life doesn't have to be drudgery. Take time for fun.

16. Work where you want to work and do what you want to do.

17. Develop a sense of humor and keep things in perspective.

18. Assume a more passive attitude by learning to be more positive and optimistic, goofing and growing. Striving for perfection is a cause of stress.

19. Be tolerant and forgiving by avoiding the bottling up of frustrations. Learn to talk out your feelings.

21. Laugh more. Show emotion. Get angry. Don't internalize your emotions. Cry, yell, scream, expend emotional energies.

22. Be sure your environmental conditions are pleasant . . . the right temperature, noise levels, and colors, can be beneficial to reducing stress.

23. Do what you want to do, not what you think others want you to do.

24. Get help if you need it. We tend to take care of the body, but not the mind. Counselors, priests, teachers, psychiatrists, psychologists are all trained to listen.

25. Be aware of your diet. Coffee, fats, oils, tea, sugar, salt, cholesterol can be unhealthly.

26. Plan time off, short periods of time. It has been found that most people do not react favorably to week long vacations. People function more effectively and experience less stress when the vacation is short . . . three or four days. Lengthy vacations stem from the good old days when it took a week to get someplace. Now travel is rapid and one does not need so much time to get there. It is difficult to slow your pace down to a "stop," as people often do, by simply lying on a beach or lounging in a hotel. Plan activities. Try to plan several "mini" vacations, rather than those two week jaunts that cause you indigestion, arguments with the family, and a burning desire to get back to work.

27. Get a medical checkup on a regular basis.

Stress can be good or harmful. Analyze your life, your health and decide what is best for you. If the stressor in your life is a person, rather than a feeling or situation, try to communicate your frustrations and talk it out. People are usually willing to listen when you make the effort. When you bottle things up, you become resentful, increasing rather than decreasing stress.

Be aware of stress. If you have a high number on the Anxiety Index and you're dealing with it, that's fine. But understand the potential outcome if nothing is done to reduce that stress.

Women and Stress

Women tend to have high psychological and physical endurance for stress. Women know more about their own feelings and are more willing to deal with emotions. However, many women, competing in a business world that's filled with men, suffer from isolation. They try to compete on the man's level, thus causing an undue amount of stress on themselves and their employees.

Homemakers can also suffer from intellectual and social isolation, which leads to depression, causing strains on family relationships and personal wellbeing. The mother who sees her family grown and her usefulness at an ebb has to deal with the questions of self worth and accomplishment.

Depression is the most common symptom of women's stress and should be dealt with the same as the other anxiety-related symptoms.

Teenage Stress

Very little has been written on the stresses of the adolescent. Much should be written, if not for the teenagers, then for the families who are also involved with the turmoil and frustrations of teen years.

Adolescence is defined as the transition from childhood to adulthood. During this period a person is supposed to progress toward mental, physical, and emotional maturity. This is a time to "find the self" and become a "human being." However, little help is given to the young, and most adults simply throw their hands up in despair as the moodiness and unpredictability of the teenager gets worse!

Anxiety for the teen manifests itself in many ways: the need for personal approval during an emotional upheaval; the guilt of sex . . . "I want to, I am physically ready, but . . ."; the guilt of not having sex when "everyone else is"; the apprehension that the hair, clothes, and general appearance is bad; the numerous choices of "good" and "bad" behavior; the need for personal intimacy and the fear; the tremendous need for peer approval — at no other time in one's life is it greater.

In addition to the anxieties, the pressures on teenagers are heavy. You must do better than Mom or Dad did in school (after all, they had to walk miles, suffer, etc); choose a life-long career (without knowing what the professional world is really like). You must succeed socially because of the pressure by parents and peers aspire to your parents' hopes and dreams; be content with the fact that maturity doesn't happen at the same rate with all people; cope with sex, even though you can't get straight answers or explanations from parents or school.

And what about internal pressures or confusion, moodiness, highs, lows, dissatisfactions, frustrations? Contrary to popular belief, teen years are not the best of life.

Today's youth have to deal with different social problems than did their parents; a world of bizarre headlines, economics, unemployment and unpredictable futures. There is more delinquency during the teen years than comparatively during later years. Rebelliousness is evident, as is the use of drugs and alcohol.

It is important for parents to understand the changes of today's youth, compared to the "good ol' days." Saying "I've been through it, and no sweat!" doesn't help the teenager to understand or solve frustrations. Open up the lines of communication. Understand the pressures and be empathetic.

Many of the same changes in life events of adults cause teenagers' stress (see Teenage Stress Test). In addition to those stressors, events such as arguments with parents, becoming involved with drugs or alcohol, suspension from school, and not being chosen for an extracurricular activity cause stress.

Adult stress-related diseases have now been found

in children, i.e., hypertension, ulcers, colds, flu, alcoholism, drug abuse, etc.

Adults oftentimes feel that "kids" have no worries. After all, teenagers don't have to pay taxes, worry about work, make heavy decisions, or "keep up with the Joneses." There are many teenagers who would disagree, as their worries and decisions are monumental.

Parents can help teenagers reduce stress by zeroing in on the problems, teaching them to relax, encouraging hobbies, doing things together (besides watching T.V.), being honest with their own feelings, having family meetings or get-togethers and just talk. The art of conversation went down the tubes (literally) with the advent of Sesame Street and Monday Night Football. Never let your child go to bed unhappy or distressed. We all need comfort, support, and sharing.

Kids — encourage your parents to communicate, then listen and weigh their advice, even though you think they are outdated with their thoughts and ideas. Try not to be pressured by your peers. Acceptance comes without having to "prove something."

Teen Stress Test

The numbered, rating scale goes from 1 to 5. Circle the appropriate number following each item.

1 - Never 2 - Only Occasionally
3 - Sometimes 4 - Frequently 5 - Always

1. Do you feel inferior to most other people?   1 2 3 4 5

2. Do you lack self-confidence?   1 2 3 4 5

3. Are you self-conscious about your appearance?   1 2 3 4 5

4. Do you often feel just miserable?   1 2 3 4 5

5. Are you often lonely?   1 2 3 4 5

6. Are you self-conscious before superiors?   1 2 3 4 5

7. Do you hesitate to volunteer in a class discussion or debate?   1 2 3 4 5

8. If you see an accident, does something keep you from giving help?   1 2 3 4 5

9. Is it hard to make up your mind until the time for action is past?   1 2 3 4 5

10. At a reception or party, do you avoid meeting the important people who are present?   1 2 3 4 5

11. Do you have an imbalance of work and recreational time?   1 2 3 4 5

12. Are you unable to work off anger and frustration physically by jogging, walking or some other form of activity?   1 2 3 4 5

13. Do you feel uncomfortable about asking others for help?   1 2 3 4 5

14. Do you endeavor to be best at everything you undertake?   1 2 3 4 5

15. Do you attempt to work on many different things in the least amount of time?   1 2 3 4 5

16. Are you uncomfortable sharing your personal thoughts, anxieties and worries with someone else?   1 2 3 4 5

17. Do you think about yourself and your problems a lot?   1 2 3 4 5

18. Do you use medication to reduce your tension, nervousness or anxiety?   1 2 3 4 5

19. Do you use alcohol to help you relax?   1 2 3 4 5

20. Is it difficult for you to philosophically accept what you cannot change?   1 2 3 4 5

Total Your Score _____

Scoring:

70-100 High Stress Level . . . You need to identify your stress generators and find more effective ways to cope with stress.

50-70 High Average . . . You are dealing with some aspects of your stress well, but need to continue looking for what generates stress for you and ways to cope more effectively.

30-50 Low Average . . . You have probably identified most generators and are coping rather effectively-keep it up!

20-30 You may be very self-assured and comfortable with yourself and your life. However, you may be in the class of people who are unaware of their stress. Remember, the first step in stress management is awareness and realistic acceptance.

Teen Alcohol Test

Let's think about teenage drinking for a moment. Drinking is often used as an escape from the stresses of reality. Abigail Van Buren ran the following test in her "Dear Abby" column. Take a few minutes to try it for yourself. *Answer yes or no.*

1. Do you lose time from school because of drinking?

2. Do you drink to lose shyness and build self-confidence?

3. Is drinking affecting your reputation?

4. Do you drink to escape from study or home worries?

5. Does it bother you if someone says that maybe you drink too much?

6. Do you have to take a drink to go out on a date?

7. Do you ever get into money troubles over buying alcoholic beverages?

8. Have you lost friends since you started drinking?

9. Do you hang out now with a crowd that gets liquor easily?

10. Do your friends drink less than you?

11. Do you drink until the bottle is empty?

12. Have you ever had a loss of memory from drinking?

13. Has drunk driving ever put you in the hospital or jail?

14. Do you get annoyed with classes or lectures on drinking?

15. Do you think you have a problem with alcohol?

If you answered "yes" to one or two questions, consider it a warning.

If you answered "yes" to three or four questions, alcohol has become a serious problem in your life. DO SOMETHING ABOUT IT NOW!

UP YOUR EFFECTIVENESS

five
**BURNOUT
OR
BURNUP?**

Burnout is a condition caused when a person works too hard for too long or endures too much stress over a short period of time. Burnout is the most severe stage of stress. Burnout is simply a depletion of personal energy. It's the sense of helplessness and hopelessness evolving from the idea that nothing can be done about problems. Burnout occurs at various rates, has different symptoms, is progressive, gets worse, and is cumulative. It is positive energy changed to negative energy. When energy is not directed to growth, the incidence of burnout increases.

Burnout can occur both in our personal lives and professional lives. We can "burnout" with our spouses, friends, kids, cars, schedule, wardrobes, pets, bosses, projects, jobs, peers, etc.

The primary causes of burnout are related to:

(a) a lack of perspective on the stresses that do occur in your life;
(2) too much responsibility, at work or in your personal life;
(3) the inability to manage your body's reaction to stress;
(4) poor time management and the inability to work effectively with other people;
(5) singlemindedness, the lack of important diversions in your life;
(6) environmental stress created by moving, divorce, business problems.

Burnout can be contagious because we become cynical, negative, pessimistic. We sometimes act the opposite of ourselves.

The impact of burnout can be acute, causing exhaustion, headaches, ulcers, sleep problems, marital upheavals, and so on.

Oftentimes super achievers, those who need to succeed and to feel successful, burnout rapidly in their personal relationships. The devotion to work and a "success" goal can be a negative for interpersonal commitments.

Burnout Phases

There are five steps to the total burnout process: *physical, social, intellectual, emotional, spiritual.* Keep in mind that we all burnout at different rates and for different reasons. We can burn out in each category each day, but remember that total burnout is like a snowball rolling down a slope . . . it gets bigger and more out of hand as it progresses. The time frame for burnout varies from person to person . . . it can take years or months depending on the person's ability to cope.

First Stage

The first stage of burnout is normally the physical. Some symptoms to look for are fatigue, "fed up" attitude, drained feeling, a minor everyday ailment becoming more noticeable and beginning to form unusual patterns such as constant backaches, neckaches or headaches.

Second Stage

The second stage of burnout is social. CPAs, lawyers, engineers, mathematicians, and computer professions will generally burnout during this stage first, rather than the physical stage. Symptoms to watch for are: putting off interaction with others, the perception of not having enough time to do things, making a commitment and not following through, irritability, decreased sexual activity. This phase can affect both work and home, whereas the physical affects home life more. It is relatively easy to get through a day of work . . . but then to come home and have to be active. No way!

Third Stage

The intellectual phase is third. You feel as if you have an information overload and just can't accept anymore facts or details; you lack attention to detail, lack concentration; your watch becomes important because you're anxious for the time to end; you begin to miss deadlines. The pattern to watch for is that, "it's not like me to be this way."

Fourth Stage

The emotional phase will find you having a very defensive attitude; "I have to get up and go to work," instead of, "I want to go to work." You ignore deadlines; there is little personal growth; you feel alienated, that everyone wants something from you and no one is meeting your needs. You are bored . . . totally and completely . . . nothing meets your approval or satisfies you. It is difficult to make decisions.

Final Stage

The final phase of the burnout process occurs when nothing has been done to remedy the other phases. It is vital to seek help if you come near this phase. You begin to question your values and feel you have little impact on life. You stop investing in people, because there is no energy or desire to do so. Other people's needs become threats and you lack any interest in making contributions to society. You become a blob!

A Solution?

We have all experienced burnout to a certain extent . . . many, total burnout. It is best to begin making positive decisions and changes when the burnout phases are experienced. Are you going in the right direction? Are your present values significant, real, realistic? Are your goals what you really want? Is your life heading in the direction you want it to, or are you living up to someone else's expectations for yourself? Take time to ask yourself these questions. Take more time when you consider the answers. So often burnout occurs because we are running feverishly in a direction we don't even care about.

The most important factor to remember about burnout is that it is a warning sign. It tells us that we are putting too much pressure on our minds and bodies, and that it is time to begin re-evaluation.

six
LIFE DESTINATIONS

Have you spent more time planning a three day weekend than your life?

What are goals? According to Websters Dictionary: the end to which a person aims to reach or accomplish. Goals can also be risks, incentives, dreams you work toward to make reality or responsibilities.

It has been proven time and time again that those who set goals achieve them, plus more. It has been found that people who consistently set goals, feel less stressed and experience less burnout frequency. People who are floating nebulously from job to job, relationship to relationship get nowhere, are bored, under a great deal of stress, prone to illness, and very unhappy. It's like the pilot that informed the passengers, after all the navigational equipment failed, that he didn't know where they were going, but since there was a tremendous tailwind, he thought a new record would be set! According to authorities, if you are moving through life, with no clear-cut sense of moving toward a specific set of goals, you are missing most of what life is all about and probably achieving only a small percentage of what you could.

Goal setting is not an easy task. Primarily you should remember to determine how you will achieve the goal. Oftentimes we set a monetary goal, but never plan how to reach it, or know who could help us, or which tools are needed.

Why do we even require goals? For one thing, goals force us to do specific things (especially if we share that goal with someone). With a goal, we can check our progress, and feel more secure. We must organize ourselves when we have goals, in order to plan daily activities.

We often only think of two categories when setting goals: career and financial. There are other categories that will give us a more balanced life such as personal goals: spiritual, community, family, and educational.

In order to reach goals, they must first be specific. Rather than saying, "I want to take a trip," think in clear-cut terms: "I will travel to Paris, France, during the month of May."

It's important for goals to have deadlines and a definite track to follow. Without a plan and a time limit for attaining a goal, the chances of accomplishing the target are unlikely.

Goals must be attainable or you might become frustrated and resentful. It isn't the end of the world if a goal is not reached, but continuous failure is demoralizing. The goals must be written down or one will lose sight of the purpose. Oftentimes ideas whiz around in our minds, but if thoughts are not written, they may be lost forever. A goal must be something you want, not something you think someone else wants of you. Forget the self-imposed obligations and let your goals be private. A goal should also be something to reach for. If the goal is too easily attainable, then lack of challenge will defeat your purpose. The goals you set should be measurable as well. Set rewards for yourself. Before you begin to write down your goals, answer these questions.

1. If I had a choice, how would I like to spend the next five years?

2. The most perfect day I could design for myself would be . . .

3. When am I really glad I'm alive?

4. How would I like to live if I knew I would be dead six months from now?

5. List five people that you admire and would most like to emulate.

6. List the things you wish had never happened.

7. How much time do you spend now with what you like most?

Those questions should give you clues as to what is really important in your life and what is not. Concentrate on those areas that you have repeated.

It is important to set both short and long term goals. Look into the future; what have you planned? If the goal for you is to be "successful," then what happens after success? Have you planned ahead for that? Have you planned for retirement?

After your goals have been written, don't just throw them in a drawer and forget about them . . . keep them in sight, look at them, change them, re-evaluate. A goal can always be changed. Don't get into the habit of being locked into one idea. As your needs and values change, so will your plans.

When we set goals, we set them for "success." Many peole reach their goals during midlife and then experience frustration and stress. It is important to establish goals beyond "success" for a richer and more fulfilled life, inasmuch as success is a journey, not a destination.

Career Change

In setting goals we often lose sight of a well rounded approach to happiness. We become locked into the security of not having to make any more major decisions. One of life's major stresses as explained in the stress chapter is boredom or lack of challenges in jobs.

Perhaps special attention should be given to career change. Earlier I mentioned that it is one thing to have a job, and another to have a career. If asked, most people in this country, and maybe even in the world, would answer that they are not happy with what they are doing for a living. Ask yourself! What's the answer? Have you ever seriously considered a change? Would you be happier doing something else? Granted, it would be a big decision.. a big step. But would you be happier in the long run? If you could rub a magic lamp, and wake up tomorrow being anything else that you wished, what would it be? Well, why don't you try to set that as a new career goal?

Impossible, you say? Well, think again! It would amaze you to see what other people are doing to change their lives for the better. Oh, it might require some real sacrifice, but maybe it would be worth it. Maybe it would require a cut in income, temporarily or permanently, but if you can figure out how to tighten the belt, that too might be worth it. After all, what is happiness worth? Consider what these people sacrificed to make their changes....

An advertising executive decided at the age of 27, when he already had two children, to go back to school and try for a career in medicine. He got his prerequisites out of the way in night school while he still worked in advertising, took his entrance exams and got accepted to medical school at the University of Missouri. He has been working for fifteen years as a General Practitioner.

A physician got burned out on the profession and started to write as an avocation and escape from the stress of his job. He started to have some real success at writing, retired from medicine, and now writes full time.

A furniture representative decided after twenty years in the business to "quit the rat race." He'd always enjoyed "playing" the stock market. One day he decided to look into becoming a broker. Finding out what the requirements were, he took a required course, passed the examination and has been happy and successful at his new profession.

An executive from one of the larger brokerage houses of the New York Stock Exchange got fed up with his stressors and started looking for a way out. He and his wife had always loved shopping for antiques and refinishing old furniture. You guessed it. They opened an antique shop, and he refinishes old furniture for others at a tidy profit. They've never been happier, even though their income is less than half what he made as an executive.

A mortician that couldn't take his work anymore sold out. With the money from the sale he bought into a travel agency. Now he travels and sees the sunnier side of life.

An elderly couple on a small pension were under stress trying to make ends meet on a fixed income, and they were going nuts trying to keep busy. Both loved travel, though they could no longer afford the luxury. They came upon the bright idea of leading tours of "golden agers" all over the world. It was an instant hit. Now they travel all over the world with people their own age and have no more trouble making ends meet.

Get the point? Now ask yourself those questions again! Come up with any interesting answers? Now do it!

seven
COPING VS. ESCAPING

There are times when we stop coping with stress and burnout. We try to escape our problems in ways that do not solve them. It is all the worse when "our way out" actually adds to the stress we already face.

One of the most common non-productive reactions to stress is overeating. Overeating in this case is defined as a consumption of food beyond that necessary to maintain good physical health. We've all had times when we ate because of "nervousness" rather than because of hunger. When such eating causes a weight problem, we've just added one more dimension to our personal stressors. Of course there are those who react just the opposite to stresses, and quit eating altogether. That can be physically even more dangerous, and reduces energies to cope at all.

Far more dangerous than over or undereating is the "escape into the bottle." Rough statistics disclose that at least one in ten of our population is alcoholic. Detection of alcoholism is very difficult because it does not strike any one distinguishable group, It takes a broad swath across the general public. Alcoholism knows no bounds. Men, women, and, tragically, children and teens become affected by this dread disease. It is a disease that affects every ethnic group, social class, economic strata, educational level. The president of the largest company or the employee on the lowest rung may be a victim of the disease. And, yes, alcoholism is a disease.

Too many of us still look upon alcoholism as a character, moral or personality problem. It is none of these. Alcoholism is a disease and as such can be controlled. Granted, it is a disease that causes weakness of character, personality changes and moral degradation, but these are symptoms, not causes. And as a disease, alcoholism can be controlled, just like diabetes, epilepsy, cardiac problems or thyroidism.

Recognizing alcoholism is a problem. Confessing to being alcoholic is difficult. Its onset is sometimes very gradual and the transition from social drinking to disease is obscured in excuses, rationalization and subjectivity.

This questionnaire, by the NATIONAL COUNCIL ON ALCOHOLISM — 733 Third Ave., New York, N.Y., will help you recognize if your drinking habits are a potential problem. Everyone should take this test, regardless of age, sex, or quantity of alcohol consumed.

CIRCLE THE BEST ANSWER FOR YOU:

Yes No 1. Do you occasionally drink heavily after a disappointment, a quarrel, or when the boss gives you a hard time?

Yes No 2. When you have trouble or feel pressure, do you always drink more heavily than usual?

Yes No 3. Have you noticed that you are able to handle more liquor than you did when you were first drinking?

Yes No 4. Did you ever wake up on the "morning after" and discover that you could not remember part of the evening before, even though your friends tell you that you did not "pass out"?

Yes   No   5. When drinking with other people, do you try to have a few extra drinks when others will not know it?

Yes   No   6. Are there certain occasions when you feel uncomfortable if alcohol is not available?

Yes   No   7. Have you recently noticed that when you begin drinking, you are in more of a hurry to get the first drink than you used to be?

Yes   No   8. Do you sometimes feel a little guilty about your drinking?

Yes   No   9. Are you secretly irritated when your family or friends discuss your drinking?

Yes   No   10. Have you recently noticed an increase in the frequency of your memory "blackouts"?

Yes   No   11. Do you often find that you wish to continue drinking after your friends say that they have had enough?

Yes   No   12. Do you usually have a reason for the occasions when you drink heavily?

Yes   No   13. When you are sober, do you often regret things you have done or said while drinking?

Yes No 14. Have you tried switching brands or following different plans for controlling your drinking?

Yes No 15. Have you often failed to keep the promises you have made to yourself about controlling or cutting down on your drinking?

Yes No 16. Have you ever tried to control your drinking by making a change in jobs, or moving to a new location?

Yes No 17. Do you try to avoid family or close friends while drinking?

Yes No 18. Are you having an increasing number of financial and work problems?

Yes No 19. Do more people seem to be treating you unfairly without good reason?

Yes No 20. Do you eat very little or irregularly when drinking?

Yes No 21. Do you sometimes have the "shakes" in the morning and find that it helps to have a little drink?

Yes No 22. Have you recently noticed that you cannot drink as much as you once did?

Yes No 23. Do you sometimes stay drunk for several days at a time?

Yes   No   24. Do you sometimes feel very depressed and wonder if life is worth living?

Yes   No   25. Sometimes after periods of drinking, do you see or hear things that aren't there?

Yes   No   26. Do you get terribly frightened after you have been drinking heavily?

If you answered "yes" to any of the questions, you have some of the symptoms that may indicate alcoholism.

"Yes" answers to several of the questions indicate the following stages of alcoholism:
Questions 1-8 Early stage
Questions 9-21 Middle stage
Questions 22-26 Beginning of final stage

eight
NON-VERBAL COMMUNICATION

UP YOUR EFFECTIVENESS

Body Language

More than 60% of communication is non-verbal!

The subconscious mind receives 75% of its messages non-verbally, so actions do speak louder than words. You project your moods, attitudes, and feelings by the way you sit, stand, and move your lips. Body language varies from culture to culture, country to country. We learn expressions from our environment, thus the variations throughout the world. There are many types of body language: social, business, athletic, romantic, etc. This chapter deals with the more formal body language of the 80's found in the American business world.

Body language is a subconscious response we don't think about it, we just react. In reading body language, the situation is very important, since more than one message can be read into a gesture. In addition, we combine many gestures to get the meaning across. An example of situation awareness would be the crossed arms on the chest: "It's cold in here and I'm trying to stay warm." "You have said or done something to put me on the defensive, so I am crossing my arms in front of me." "I am feeling fat and trying to cover up." "This is just a comfortable position I feel relaxed in." Be aware of the situation and let your intuition help you. Remember we are dealing with the subconscious.

Handshakes:

It is easiest to begin with the handshake. It is usually the first contact we have with someone, in business and socially. It is important for both a man and a woman to extend their hands to shake in a business situation. This establishes the business atmosphere and rapport. It is appropriate for a gentleman to extend his hand to the lady and appropriate ladies, to extend your hand to the gentleman, and to another lady as well.

There are several handshakes to watch for:

FIRM, WITH EYE TO EYE CONTACT — this person is self-confident, ready to do business, honest.

FIRM, WITH EYES DROPPING TOWARD THE FLOOR — lacking self-confidence, hiding something.

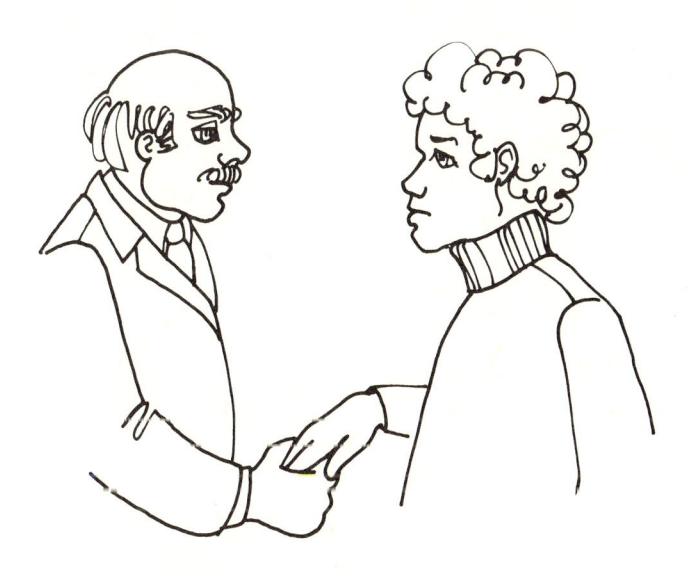

FISH SHAKE — limp and unassuming, if this person doesn't have an arthritic condition, he is showing apathy, and little enthusiasm.

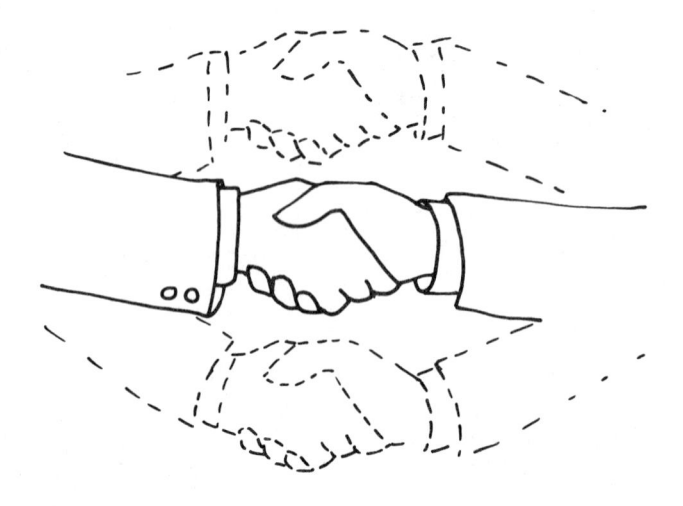

PUMPER — the person who continues to shake your hand after a few seconds, unwilling to let go is saying that he wants control. Oftentimes people are afraid of losing your attention if they let go of your hand.

HALF SHAKE — this can be a very condescening shake, with the person only giving you half his hand, and saying through non-verbal communication that you only deserve half the respect from him. Oftentimes, however, a gentleman doesn't know whether to shake a lady's hand or not and consequently will give the half shake.

GODZILLA GRIP — when the ring on your right hand is indented into all of your fingers. This person is showing power, strength and frequently a macho attitude. Sometimes one does not know his own strength!

TURNING THE HAND OVER — the person who turns the hand over has a desire to control and dominate. Next time you experience this shake, try to casually turn the hand back over; the shaker will sub-consciously turn your hand back over to remain in the domineering position.

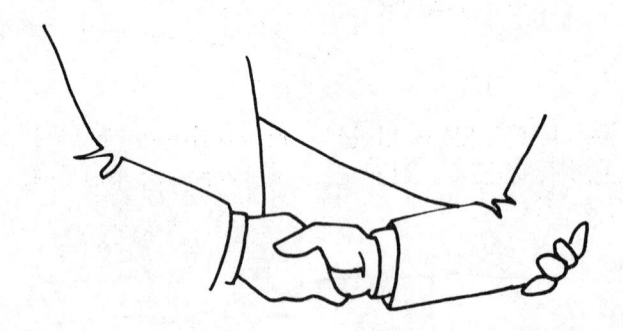

HAND TO ELBOW — this can mean one of two things . . . it can be a very warm and sincere shake, "Gee, it's good to see you again," or, it can mean, "I'm gonna get you!" Frequently people will pull you into their territory or "space" when they feel they need to control. This can be accomplished with the hand to elbow shake.

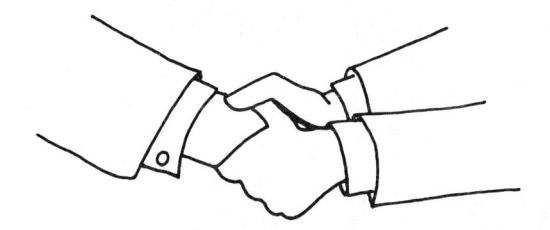

HAND OVER HAND — much the same as the hand to elbow. This can be warm or intimidating.

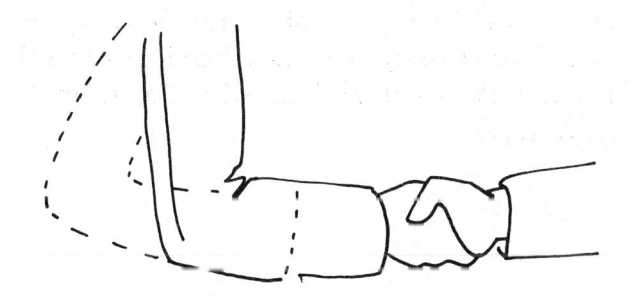

JERKING AND NOT LETTING GO — this person is saying, "Come to me, I will not come to you." It is a form of power and control.

SWEATY PALMS — nervousness and anxiety. When we start to come to a decision our palms will often sweat.

The position of the arms and hands can indicate feelings ranging from frustration or doubt to happiness and acceptance. Watch for how others hands and arms receive you. Learn what they can tell you before the other person even opens his or her mouth.

ARMS AT SIDES, FISTS CLENCHED — this shows that the person is coming to a decision, either negative or positive; showing anxiety.

PALMS DOWN — this is a negative sign; expect to meet resistance. When a person says he really likes something, and the gesture is palms down — don't believe him!

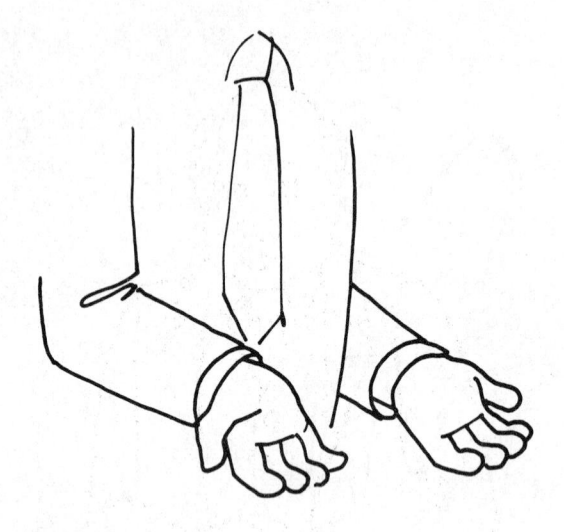

PALMS UP — a positive sign; they are ready to go! Try an experiment . . . put your palms up as if you were gesturing, and say "no" . . . palms down as if you were gesturing, say "yes." Does it feel right? It shouldn't. Often people in my workshops question the baseball gesture of "safe," and wonder why palms down is negative . . . who is getting the negative signal? The player who did not get the runner out! Negative!

TRIANGLE or PYRAMID — this gesture is most interesting in that you can tell if someone is feeling self-confident or superior to you. Any time you see the triangle, you are seeing superiority. Keep in mind that this is a subconscious response . . . there's nothing wrong with it; just bear in mind where the person is coming from . . . or if you are using the triangle . . . where are you coming from? The higher the pyramid, the more superior the person is feeling.

HANDS IN FRONT OF WAIST — humble superiority.

HANDS TOGETHER ON FACE — superior evaluation.

ARMS BEHIND HEAD — extreme self-confidence. This person will be difficult to communicate with in this position, as he thinks he knows everything there is to know. He may listen, but probably won't change his mind. One of the best ways to handle this person, if he is behind a desk (normally with one foot on a drawer or part of the desk) is to put something such as paper, a folder, pen, or briefcase on his desk. By doing this you will probably bring him forward out of the superior position. Leaning on the desk can also have the same effect. The terms "territory" and "space" have been twice mentioned and will be discussed later in this chapter.

HANDS ON HIPS — (with feet relaxed), relaxed and superior.

HANDS ON HIPS — (with weight on forward foot), stubborn stance.

ONE HAND ON HIP — relaxed or snobby stance.

NOSE ITCHING — during uncomfortable situations we find ourselves scratching our nose.

TILT OF HEAD — evaluation, when the head goes up the decision is made.

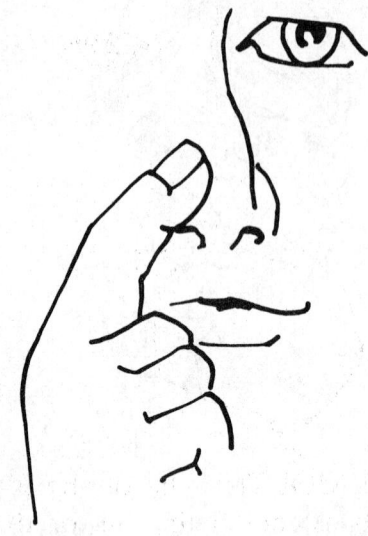

RUBBING NOSE — doubt. If the rubbing occurs when you are talking (rubbing your own nose) you doubt what you are saying. If you are talking and your listener rubs his nose, he's doubting what you are saying.

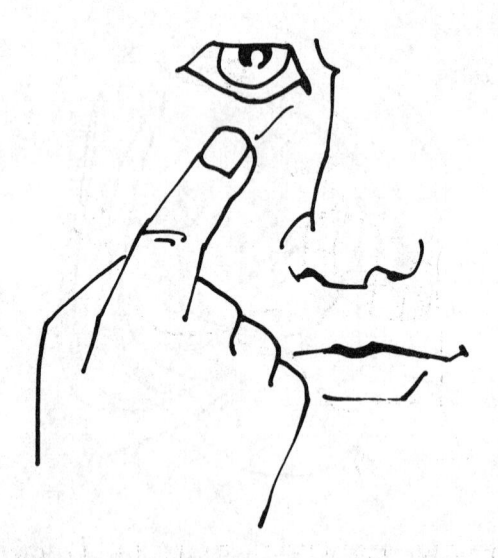

RUBBING UNDER THE EYE — doubt.

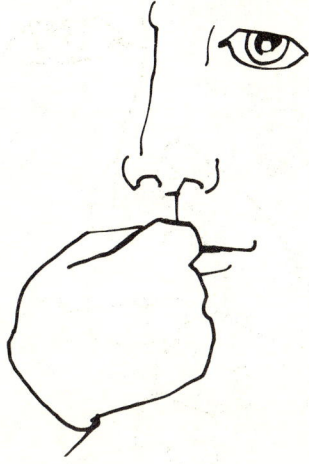

HAND ON MOUTH — he or she is holding something back, not telling all, or this could mean doubt. Depending on how long the hand stays at the mouth can indicate whether the gesture is doubt or evaluation . . . during evaluation, the hand *stays* on the mouth.

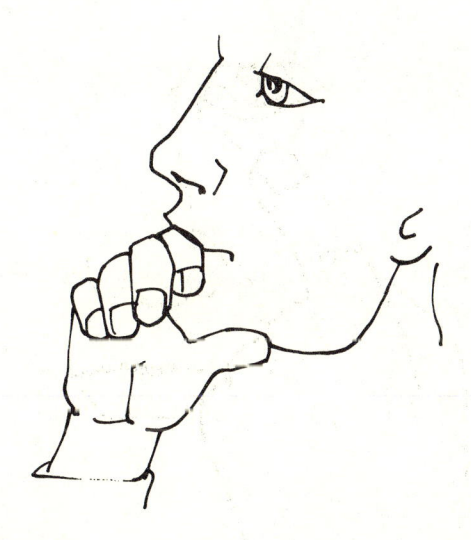

HAND ON MOUTH, THUMB LOCKED UNDER CHIN — total resistance.

HAND ON FOREHEAD — concern and/or evaluation . . . this generally indicates a thought process.

PINCHING BRIDGE OF NOSE — great concern.

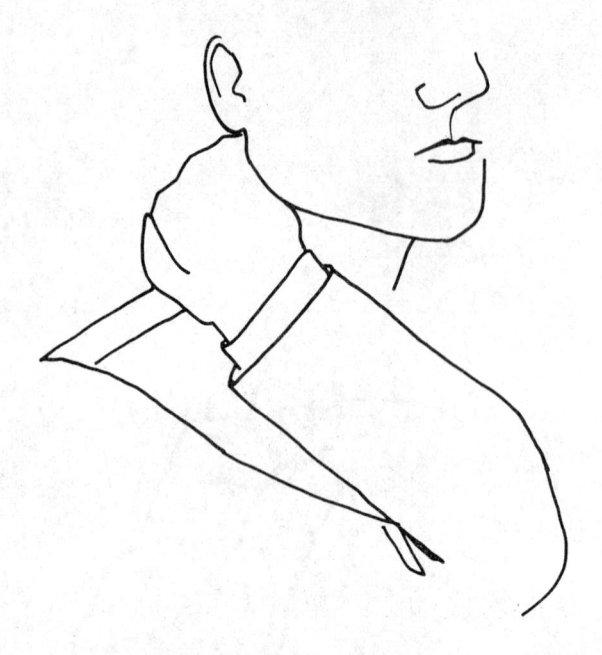

HAND TO NECK/PINCHING FLESHY PART OF HAND — seeking reassurance . . . tell this person that the decision is good or that everything will be fine.

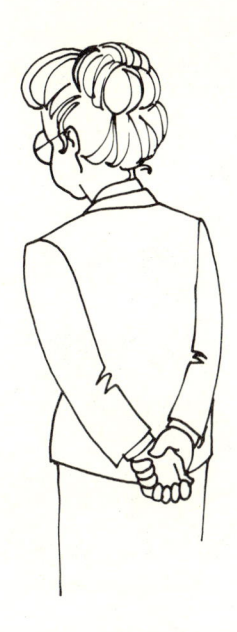

ARMS BEHIND BACK — humbleness

OPEN POSITION — positive and receptive — anytime an arm crosses the body or the legs cross, the person becomes less receptive, as he goes into a protective stance.

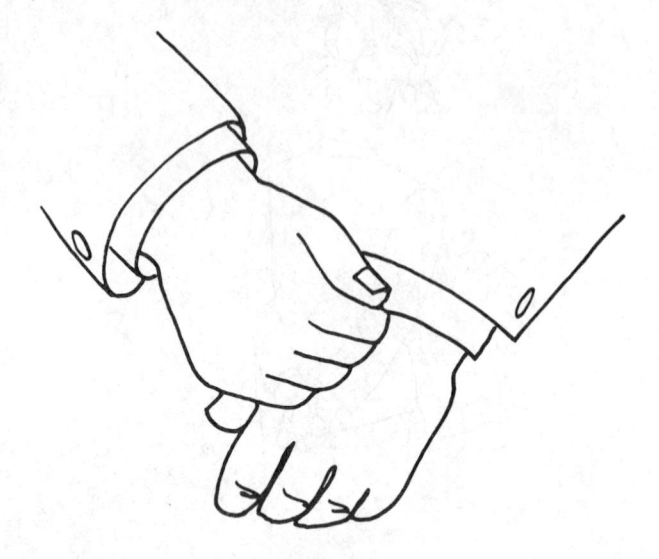

PLAYING WITH OR PULLING ON A CUFF, WATCH, BUTTON (on coat or sleeve), or SEAM — protectiveness to oneself. This person is feeling intimidated and insecure. Give him more physical space (back away) or ease up on your verbal presentation.

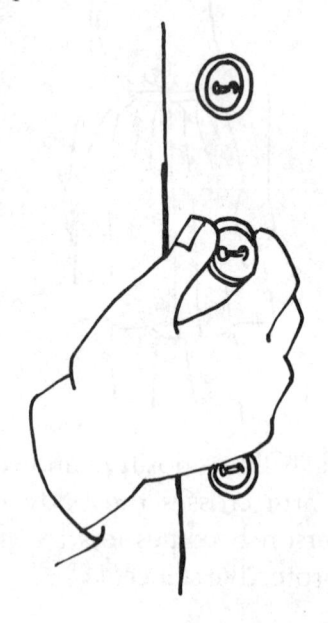

HANDS IN POCKETS — relaxed or protective

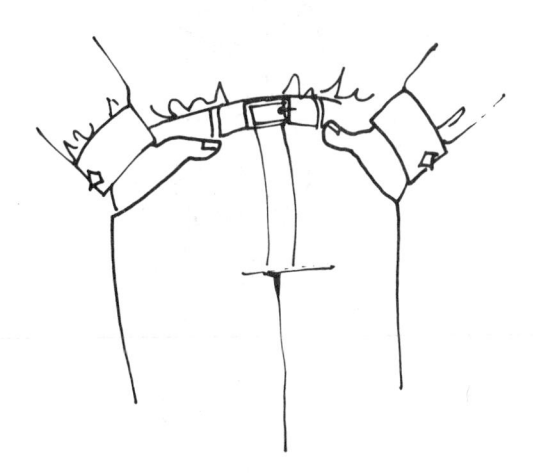

HANDS IN POCKETS WITH THUMBS OUT
— superiority

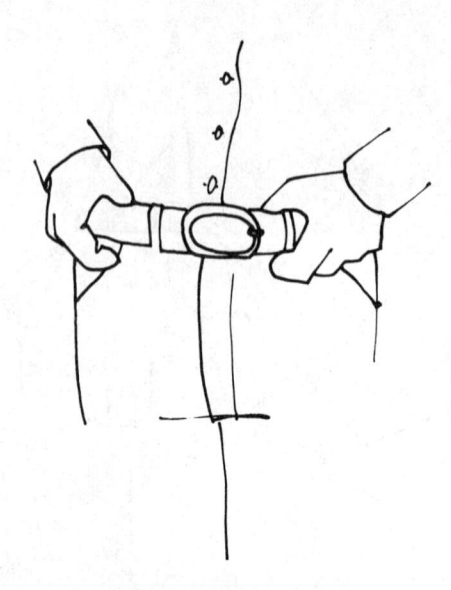

THUMBS IN BELT, POCKET — macho! The ego is showing.

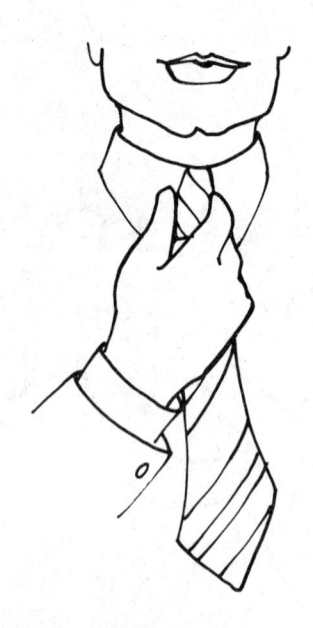

PLAYING WITH TIE KNOT — frustration/anxiety - social flirtation

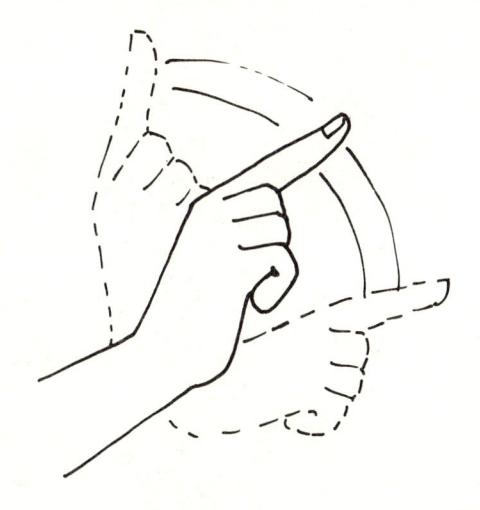

POINTED FINGER/SHAKING FINGER —
anxiety and authority

CHIN RESTING ON HAND — thinking posture

THUMB UNDER CHIN HOLDING MOUTH CLOSED — resistance in thought

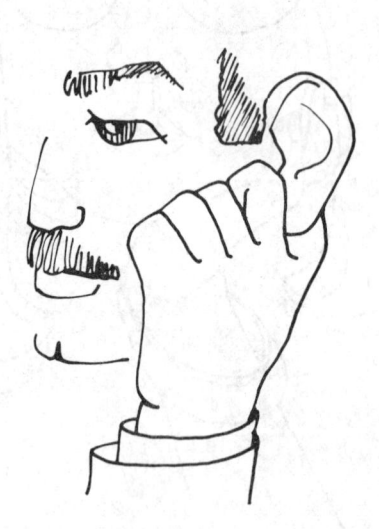

PULLING EAR — "I heard your question and I'm thinking about it." Typical masculine gesture.

TWISTING THE HAIR — nervousness, a flirtation, stalling. Typical feminine gesture.

CROSSED ARMS WITH CLENCHED FISTS — anger. Hand this person something to get him out of the defensive position, and to generate an attitude change, if only for a few seconds.

BUTTONED COAT/JACKET — protectiveness or defensiveness

UNBUTTONED COAT/JACKET — open, relaxed, receptive

TAPPING FINGERS/PLAYING WITH RINGS, NECKLACE, WATCH, JEWELRY — boredom, impatience

LOOKING AT WATCH — people look at a watch to see how much time is left, not what the actual time is. Ask someone who has just looked at his watch, the correct time . . . he will have to look again to answer you. Looking at watch could also mean impatience or boredom.

TAPPING FINGERS RAPIDLY — impatience/boredom.

Seated Positions:

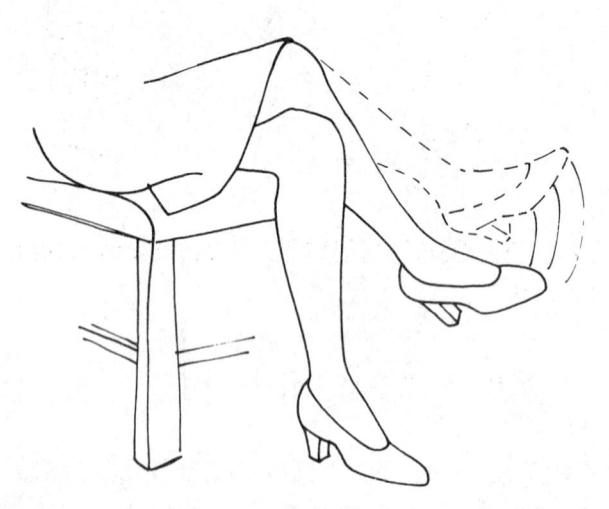

SWINGING OF LEG — rapidly — impatience, "Let's get on with it."
SWINGING OF LEG — slowly — flirtation.

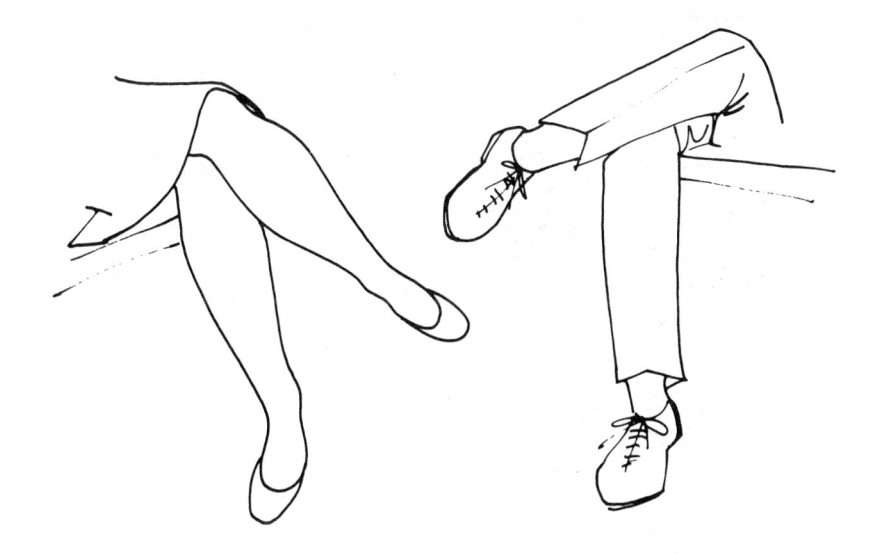

LEG CROSSED TO YOU — open and receptive to you

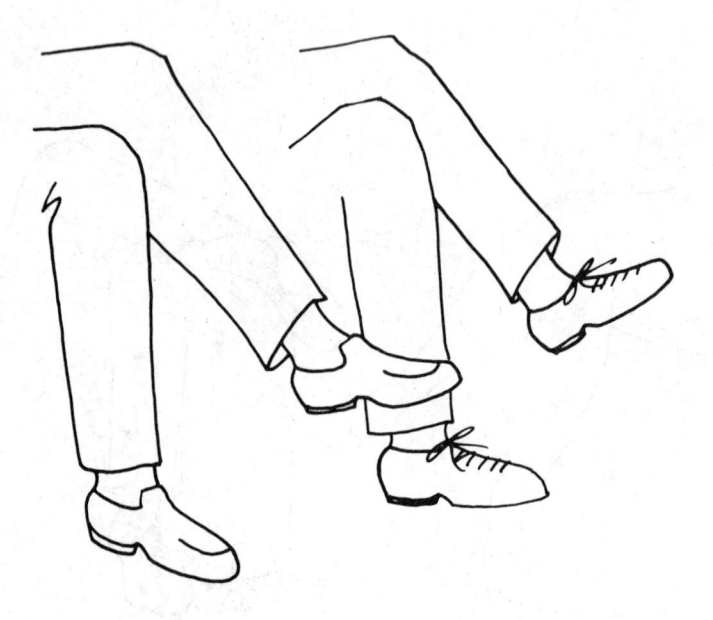

LEG CROSSED AWAY FROM YOU — closed to you and your ideas. When two people are in agreement their crossed legs will be toward one another. As they disagree you will see a slight shift in their posture and the legs will uncross, and recross away from one another.

"LINCOLN" POSITION — open and receptive
(great for a job interview)

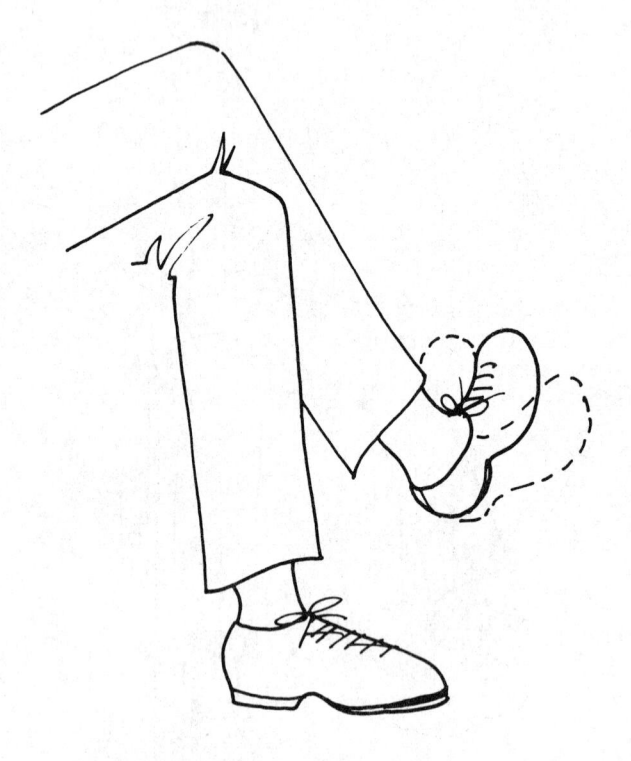

ROTATING THE FOOT QUICKLY — boredom and impatience

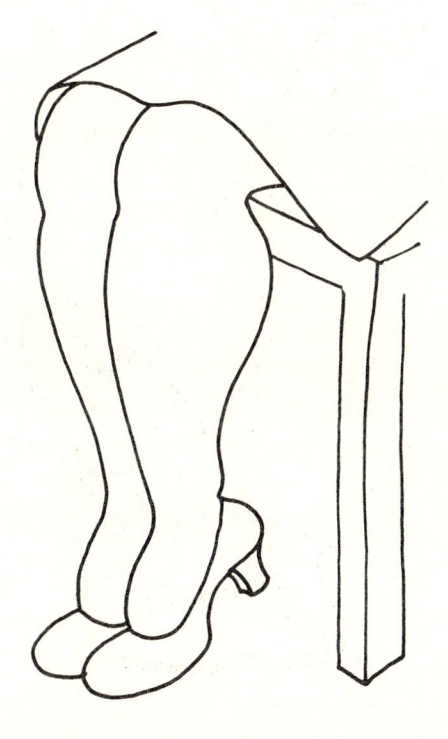

ON TIP OF TOES — (feet are tucked under chair and the pressure is on the toes) — undivided attention and interest

Space and Territory...

Everyone needs a certain amount of space surrounding themselves. We all have a favorite chair, place at the table, favorite route to take, one that we consider just "ours." We resent anyone using or taking that space. As long as there is optional space, most people will tend to sit as far from strangers as possible, especially on a bus on in a lecture hall. The way in which we use space communicates. A whisper in someone's ear is close proximity, whereas a shout across the room tells us something else. We feel cramped and uncomfortable if crowded. We feel best with between 18-36 inches of space between us and the next person. Take, for example, people standing in line at a cafeteria or theater; they are evenly spaced.

During a social occasion, we can deal with less space, as little as 8 to 10 inches between us, but how do we stand? — with a drink or cigarette in our hands or using the crossed arm position.

People on elevators are a wonderful example of the importance of space. People do one of two things on an elevator . . . watch the numbers of the floors or analyze the fiber in the carpet. In an elevator there is no room to move and some people feel extremely uncomfortable.

There are three special territories we all have: social, personal, and intimate. We establish territories in different ways, depending on the situation. Space requirements are different for individuals . . . some need more, some less. In a personal situation such as sitting at a table in a restaurant, people will move the silverware, ashtray, salt and pepper shakers, ketchup bottle, to establish a territory. If that territory is invaded by another's water glass, plate or silverware one will physically move it back, but think about it subconsciously. In a classroom you may put papers, pens, briefcases, folders, and personal items, around your space without knowing or thinking about it. We feel uncomfortable if someone moves our items, or puts their own possessions close to ours. People who sit at the end of a table need more space than others, and will almost always take an end chair. Note your setting now. How have you established your territory? How have your family and work associates established territories?

Some people will try to establish territory by standing very close to you when they talk . . . nose to nose! These people are either presuming intimidation or trying to maintain control by using your territory. Do not move away from these people, since you will be giving in to their power structure. Stand your ground and watch them reluctantly move back.

Offices use space to distribute power. In Europe, many people are likely to put their desks in the center of the room, thus having the authority flow outward from the center. In America, it's the "office at the top" . . . the large spacious penthouse suite, with authority flowing downward. Americans will also distribute their authority around the edges of the room by placing the desks to the outside.

Touch

Another invasion of space and territory is touch. Often people are intimidated and put off by touching during business conversations. Touching can be good, reassuring, even healing, except to those who have not grown up in a touching atmosphere, or those who only casually know the toucher. There are many different types of touches, the most common being the arm grabber, shoulder poker, knee slapper, back slapper, elbow pincher. "Touchers" generally do not know they are reaching out during conversations . . . be aware if you are a toucher; people could back away from you.

The Stall

There is another type of non-veral communication people use, the "Stall." When people are trying to think, come up with an answer, or don't know an answer, several gyrations are used. Chewing the end of the pen is one and can also be related to evaluation. Other stalls are stroking the beard or face, lighting a cigarette, cigar or pipe (pipe smokers have the best stall techniques of any . . . as they clean, pack, rearrange, etc.), inspecting fingernails, twisting hair, pulling on the ear lobe, staring into space. Silence is one of the most effective stalls, forcing the other party to become uncomfortable and perhaps intimidated.

Eyes

The eyes are constantly moving because of the sensory processing that is taking place. Don't be alarmed when someone's eyes move during a conversation . . . it is a thought process. The eyes move upward when visualization is taking place, remain level throughout the auditory process, and move downward during emotional processing.

People use the mouth to mask emotion, but they can't cover up their underlying emotions in facial expression above the nose.

Eyes staring into space and not focused, with some pupil dilation: Either visual recall or visualizing something that has never been seen before.

Eyes horizontal, looking right or left: Making sense of sounds one is at the moment, recalling sounds from memory, imagining sounds — auditory processing.

Eyes down and to the right: Sensing how the body feels — processing kinesthetic input.

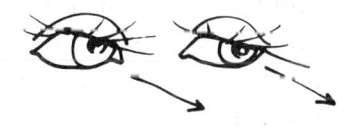

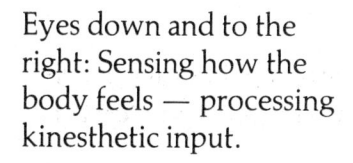

Eyes down and to the left: Talking to oneself — an internal dialogue in the auditory mode.

Eye Watching

Eye movements are linked to the kind of sensory processing that is going on in a person at any given moment. The eye patterns and readings for a right-handed person are seen below. The eye movement may be only a bare flicker, or it may be held for several seconds. The individual may be organizing incoming current sensations, recalling others from the past, or imagining still others never previously experienced. In all cases, one gets clues to whether the mode of processing is visual, auditory, or kinesthetic (involving stimuli generated within the body itself) by watching the eyes.

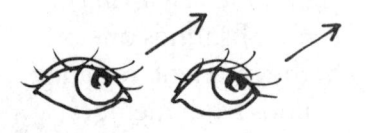

Eyes up and to the left: Recalling something seen before — a visual memory.

Eyes up and to the right: Visualizing something that has not been seen before.

Power

Another aspect of non-verbal communication is the projection of power exhibited in various ways. Earlier I mentioned the handshakes indicating power . . . hand over hand, hand to elbow, turning the hand over, as well as the intimidating touch. Power is seen in stance as well. The slouching person is obviously not self confident or assertive, while the counterpart, the "standing tall" individual will assert more authority. One who stands with both feet planted firmly, is exhibiting power, as opposed to one who tucks a leg around the other and seems off balance. There are material indications of power as well, as large desk in an office, the tall chair behind the desk and the small chairs in front of the desk.

Power is also indicated by the person behind the desk, leaning back in the chair with a foot on the desk or drawer. Sitting in the small chairs in front of the desk, you are immediately in a condescending position, inasmuch as the person behind the desk is sitting higher, looking down at you. The "ego wall" behind the desk, containing awards, plaques, and trophies, is a symbol of power.

A briefcase is a strong symbol of power, a black case being the most intimidating. If you feel you need extra help for a powerful and authoritative image, use a briefcase, but keep it subtle, of soft leather, and light color.

The pen you use indicates how you feel about your image of power. In a business transaction why use a $.25 pen that smudges, skips, and ultimately runs out of ink? Use a heavy, attractive pen. It doesn't have to be expensive. People will be impressed and more willing to use the "important" pen. As an executive, people will be constantly evaluating you. Complete your image with the proper accoutrements!

Incidentally, gentlemen, your tie is a symbol of power and can be devastating if your spouse casually picks it out for you, or if you arbitrarily select the first one on the rack. People's eyes are drawn to the tie and within seconds will evaluate your status and decision-making abilities. Use simple stripes, sophisticated polka-dots, or plain colors to enhance the power image. Avoid ties that have pictures, stories, or shiny surfaces.

Silence is power. One can state many moods, attitudes, and feelings by not saying a word. It is often said that after a question is asked, the first person to speak loses. What are you telling someone when he says "good morning" and you don't respond? When someone asks you a question and you don't respond? Do you use silence to anger someone during an argument? Do you use it as stubbornness? Silence can be cold, bitter, and build walls. When used appropriately, silence can emphasize, get people's attention and put you in the limelight by being a good listener, a thoughtful person.

Listening

I categorize listening as a form of non-verbal communication, even though many don't practice it as such. Television has nearly ruined our listening habits. We have learned to tune out, daydream, ignore. There are several factors that inhibit the listening process; awareness of those will help you become a better listener.

We often "hear" what people say, rather than "listen." Hearing is the act of receiving and perceiving sounds. We "hear" many sounds around us . . . stop and "hear" them now . . . but we don't dwell on them. "Listening" is simply hearing with a purpose.

During a listening situation you must be aware of the picture or interpretation the speaker conjures up in the mind of the listener. We all visualize words, but in different ways, i.e., the word "horse" can be pictured as, brown, black, standing in a pasture, running in the wind, a palomino, a race horse, a white horse feeding, etc.

In addition to varying pictures we must remember that people, at any given time, wear different "hats."

A person can interpret differently according to the particular hat he is wearing at the time. Think of how differently the word "money" would be interpreted by a person wearing the hat of: a churchgoer, a voter, a driver, a golfer, a car owner, a stockholder, an employee, a father, an uncle, a music lover, a taxpayer, a consumer, a card player, a football fan, a husband, a gambler.

Communication is a two way process. We need to put ourselves in the listener's/speaker's place in order to avoid communication breakdown.

More effective listening is accomplished by becoming aware of the listening barriers we confront. Some of the more obvious barriers are:

Impatience — our thoughts zoom ahead of the speaker and we are anxious to get on with the conversation.

Stress — it is difficult to concentrate when our stress levels are high.

Criticizing the speaker's delivery — we often spend time analyzing the speaker's clothing, makeup and hair, rather than paying attention to the words.

Evading the difficult — our mind will skirt the difficult, thus breaking the thought and listening process.

Resistance to the topic and/or speaker — sometimes we don't like the subject matter or the speaker and stop listening or concentrating.

Self-preoccupation or polyphasia — the flight of idea or thoughts can distract us from the speaker.

Concern with non-essentials — such as the color of the room, someone across the room, the whir of the air conditioner, etc.

Color of the room — can be distracting and unsettling.

Personality conflict — when you don't like a personality you stop listening.

Time — feeling rushed or bored. Too much time given to subject matter.

Tone of voice — a pleasing tone is much easier to listen to than harshness.

Beliefs — both yours and the speaker's influence listening capacity.

Physical and mental health — if you're having a bad day, listening will be restrained.

Appearance — it only takes 7 to 10 seconds for someone to decide if they like you or not. It is easier to listen to someone you like! Someone may not like the colors you are wearing, the style, the hair or makeup, shoes or glasses. All these will affect how people listen to you.

Vocabulary — each person has certain "emotional" words that turn them off or make them uncomfortable. When these words are heard, the mind reacts, taking away from listening ability.

Listening Test

Try the following "Listening Test" to see how accurately you listen. Have a member of your family or a friend give you the following questions. Answers should be written. Questions should be read once, *and not repeated.*

1. In the series of numbers, 82154, the second number is:

2. In the series of numbers, 90132, the odd number next to the last is:

3. In the series of numbers, 521076, the third number is:

4. Of the words school and box, write the shorter word.

5. Write no, even if you think cows are larger than dogs.

6. List the numbers 2, 7, 9, 5, and 8 and circle the largest.

7. (Referring to the above question) If you circled 7 make a square, if not make a cross.

8. Give the wrong answer to this question: Are you in the United States?

9. If you went to bed at 8:00 PM and set the manual alarm to get you up at 9:00, how many hours of sleep would you get?

10. Does England have a 4th of July?

11. Why can't a man living in Denver, Colorado, be buried in a spot east of the Mississippi River?

12. Some months have 30 days, some have 31, how many have 28 days?

13. If a doctor gave you 3 pills and told you to take one every half hour, how long would they last you?

14. A man builds a house with four sides to it. It is a rectangular shape. Each side has a southern exposure. A big bear wanders by. What color is the bear?

15. A farmer had 17 sheep, all but 9 died, how many did he have left?

16. Divide 30 by one half, add ten, what is the answer?

17. How many animals of each species did Moses take aboard the ark?

18. If you take 2 apples from 3 apples, what do you have?

19. A woman gives a beggar $2.00. The woman is the beggar's sister, but the beggar is not the woman's brother. Why?

20. If you entered a dark room and you had a match, a candle, and an oil lamp, which would you light first?

Answers

1. (2)
2. (3)
3. (1)
4. The word "box" should be WRITTEN not printed.

5. The word "no" should be WRITTEN not printed.
6. A "list" is either horizontal (2, 7, 9, 5, 8) or vertical.
7. If "7" was circled a square should have been made or a cross . . . not an X.
8. no
9. 1 hour
10. Yes, England has a 1st of July, 2nd, 3rd, etc.
11. He is still alive.
12. All of them. (Most people who miss #10 will also miss this question. We tend to be preconditioned to thinking of February with 28 days . . . when the question is asked the mind races to February and doesn't think of the other months, all of which have 28 days and more.)
13. 1 hour . . . start at 12:00 for the first pill, 12:30 for the second, 1:00 for the last.
14. The key is ALL SIDES HAVING A SOUTHERN EXPOSURE, the house is at the North Pole and the bear is white.
15. He still had 9.
16. 70 . . . when you divide by a fraction you invert and multiply . . . many people will hear "divide IN half", rather than "divide BY half."
17. Zero . . . it wasn't Moses . . . this question is a perfect example of assumption . . . you may have heard "Moses", but thought the speaker meant Noah, or all you heard was "animals and ark."
18. You still have 2 apples . . . the question did not read, "What do you have left?"
19. The beggar is a woman . . . we often have preconceived ideas about subjects . . . how do you picture a beggar . . . as a woman?
20. You would have to light the match before being able to light anything else.

This was just to give you an idea of your listening capabilities . . . it doesn't matter how many you missed. Be aware of your weak points.

Better Listening

There are several simple and easy ways to improve your listening habits. First of all, limit your own talking; try not to interrupt, hear people thru; don't jump to conclusions, respond instead of reacting. Use logic instead of emotion. Turn off your worries and pay attention to what the speaker is saying. Instead of saying "yeah" use the word "yes" . . . it takes more muscles and concentration to say "yes" . . . you will automatically become a better listener when using "yes." Be open-minded. Search for feelings expressed by asking questions. Be aware of your own attitudes.

A good listener automatically becomes a better communicator, and lessens the stress of others by being more empathetic.

UP YOUR EFFECTIVENESS

nine
PSYCHOLOGICAL EFFECTS OF COLOR

We communicate powerfully with color, and are affected subconsciously by clothing and environmental color. Color is energy . . . some colors give us energy, some take it away. Our personalities show up in the colors we select to wear, the cars we buy, and the decorating we do at home and in the office. Color affects our attitudes, mood and physical well-being. We aren't usually conscious of our surrounding colors, yet we experience the sensation of the effect of them. Emotionally, colors have a tremendous impact. Have you ever walked into a room, felt uncomfortable, and didn't know why? There is a good chance the colors affected you. If you tend to be moody around the house . . . change the color scheme, and watch your attitude change. Industries have found that color changes not only affect moods, but increase production, improve quality of work, reduce eye strain, and reduce absenteeism.

Stress and Color

Overstimulation, from colors, as well as monotony may cause stress and distress. White is especially bad under high illumination. Red can raise the blood pressure, cause uneasiness, and excitement. Red can do as much for you under some circumstances, as can a strong drink.

We all react to color . . . we just react with different intensities. You have to get to know your own limitations. Research shows that even color blind people respond to the energy of colors.

Moods of people are changed by environment . . . beauty and ugliness, sunny or rainy weather. People in bright, sunny settings seem to be better dispositioned. If you are prone to moodiness, use the warm colors . . . red, orange, beige.

Colors of Work Areas

In a work area, it has been found that white causes eye fatigue. If muscular work is to be done, bright colors (orange, yellow, coral) should be used. A sedentary task needs reduced brightness to avoid distraction, use green, blue, beige.

Red may be used for a short period of time to generate ideas, but if used too long, overstimulation and uneasiness will occur.

People in a blue room will be sluggish, and rates of thought process and activity will decrease. One can easily implement ideas in a room decorated in light green. Yellow can cause eye strain and little thought process if it is bright. Use a green background to develop ideas.

The intensity of the color has a lot to do with our reactions to that particular color. Colors may be stimulating to one and passive to another.

If a work area is warm, use cool colors. Use warm colors to compensate for the lack of natural light and to warm a chilly place. Where distractions are to be avoided, as in the think tank, use light greens and grays. Bright yellow, which increases visibility is best for stairways in work areas.

Relief from fatigue is found with soft colors. Eight hours of surgery couldn't be performed in a red room.

Animals/Color

Animals react to colors, too. It was found in a zoo that the white monotonous walls made the animals lethargic, withdrawn, and non-propagative. The environmental colors were changed and so were the actions of the animals. They became more energetic.

If you prefer one color on your walls, be sure to use accent colors to interrupt the monotony, or you too may become lethargic and withdrawn.

Color vs. Visibility

The most visible color combination is black on yellow, then green on white, red on white, blue on white, white on blue, black on white. Isn't it interesting that most printed matter is black on white?

Moods/Color

One of the reasons we react to color is that we associate colors with mental and emotional impressions. Therefore, color can have a contradictory effect. As an example, the color black can be associated with darkness, emptiness, death, mourning or sophistication.

The moods conveyed by colors can be very diverse.

There has been much written about the effects of pink, a subduing color. Many criminal institutions use a pink room to relax aggressive behavior; schools are doing the same. A person in a pink room will be receptive and relaxed within 30 minutes. That's because exposure to pink causes muscle strength to diminish, the heartbeat slows, and the person calms down.

Would the color pink, as related to "baby girls," have anything to do with a girl's strength, as she grows up? Some researchers feel it does, thus enabling boys, who get the blue blankets, rooms, booties, and clothes, to be stronger.

Because color affects our emotions, so it affects our digestive systems as well. Have you ever eaten from an odd colored plate? What was your reaction? Have you ever eaten "blue" food? Ordinarily it is not an appetizing color. The most appealing colors are red, orange, yellow, with yellow-green being the least appealing.

As for mood, the exciting colors are deep orange, yellow, and scarlet. Tranquilizing colors are light yellow, and green. Subduing colors are the spiritual colors, violet and purple. Light colors are passive and the bright, active.

Personalities and Color

Personalities are shown by the colors we select and surround ourselves with. We are talking about choice of colors, not in clothing, but in decor. We select different colors in clothing for our "business personality," as opposed to our "at home, relaxed personality."

The selection of red in the environment indicates aggressiveness, or the need to be aggressive. It has been found that when surrounded by red the blood pressure rises . . . Introverts have difficulty relating to red because of the warm and exciting sensations emitted by the color. People who are fond of red most often like action, are outspoken, fickle, athletic, quick-tempered, and tend to make instantaneous decisions. Those who dislike red have a strong desire to get out of the "rat race," seek security, escape from themselves and the world, and want a secluded home.

An authoritative and powerful color is blue, helping one gain control of a situation. The preference toward blue in decorating indicates resourcefulness, sensitivity toward others, and untapped capabilities. The "blue" person may internalize emotions and be unduly serious, opinionated and stubborn. The person who dislikes blue is likely to envy success in others and be resentful. In addition, this person may lack stability in himself, and be wary of having to concentrate for any length of time. The person who decorates a room in blue will probably dictate the household, and be the decision maker.

Green is the soothing color, the healing color. In fact, a green household can be so relaxing that the inhabitants become overweight. Get rid of your green refrigerator if you're trying to diet. Those who like green tend to be active in the community, wanting to be liked, in addition to over-indulging themselves. To dislike green indicates the desire for city life and reluctance for small town living.

Orange is the color favored by top sales people, bankers and lawyers. This is the person who loves money, parties, and the fast lane . . . a friendly person, able to get along with almost everyone, dislikes being alone. The person who dislikes orange likely cringes at vigorous hand shaking and backslapping. This person is usually tied in many knots which are difficult to loosen, and probably is seeking companionship.

The conservative personality will select the earth tones for his surroundings, especially brown. This is the person who is normally dependable, takes life seriously and is amused by the flighty ways of others. Sometimes this person's discipline may be difficult for others to accept. He tends to be quick-witted, but has little patience with anything that requires undue effort and hard labor.

Yellow is the color of the high-minded and intellectual. The "yellow" person will probably have a controlled temper, but may be stubborn about changing his mind. The disliking of yellow indicates a person that has little patience with anything involved or complex. He probably prides himself on sound judgment and common sense.

People who surround themselves with orchid are creative, highly intelligent, intuitive and have a spiritual presence. The negative side shows vanity and lack of follow-thru.

White indicates a person with low vitality. Remember how white reflects and causes fatigue?

Gray suggests that the decorator is seeking composure and indicates one who is cautious. The gray person is intelligent, loyal, and shows some sophistication.

Gold implies cheerfulness, intelligence, a balanced personality, kindness and conservatism.

UP YOUR EFFECTIVENESS

ten
I'D PICK MORE DAISIES

It is difficult to summarize a book that is so diversified and personal as this.

I feel it is vitally important to know one's self in order to be happy, successful, and a good communicator. If you are able to use only one idea from this text, you have spent your time effectively, growing and expanding your horizons.

As a public speaker and educator I have always concluded my presentations with some poignant thoughts written by Nadine Stair. The poem summarizes my feelings about who we are, where we're going, and how to get there. Its philosophy will UP YOUR EFFECTIVENESS . . .

I'd Pick More Daisies

by Nadine Stair

If I had my life to live over,
   I'd try to make more mistakes next time.
I would relax,
   I would limber up,
I would be sillier than I have been this trip.
I know of very few things I would take seriously.
I would be crazier,
   I would be less hygenic,
I would take more chances
I would take more trips,
   Climb more mountains,
Swim more rivers
   And watch more sunsets.

I would burn more gasoline.
I would eat more ice cream and fewer beans.
I would have more actual problems,
   and fewer imaginary ones.

You see, I am one of those people
   Who live prophylactically and sensibly and sanely,
Hour after hour, day after day.
Oh, I have had my moments,
   And if I had it to do over again,
I'd have more of them.
In fact I'd have nothing else,
   Just moments, one after another,
Instead of living so many years ahead of each day.

I have been one of those people
   Who never goes anywhere without a thermometer,
   A hot water bottle, a gargle, a raincoat and
     a parachute.

If I had it to do over again,
   I would go places and do things
And travel lighter than I have.

If I had my life to live over,
   I would start barefoot earlier in the Spring
And stay that way later in the Fall.

I would play hooky more.
I wouldn't make such good grades except by accident.
I would ride on more merry-go-rounds.

I'D PICK MORE DAISIES.